TEARING DOWN WALLS

A Woman's Triumph

Mary Gardiner Jones

To Elizabeth
whose walls to be torn down
were much higher and thicker and whose only
tools were her southern culture of
tenderness and politeness — that she
managed and is admired and respected
by all her friends and colleagues,
Mary

Hamilton Books
A member of
The Rowman & Littlefield Publishing Group
Lanham · Boulder · New York · Toronto · Plymouth, UK

Hamilton Books
4501 Forbes Boulevard
Suite 200
Lanham, Maryland 20706
Hamilton Books Acquisitions Department (301) 459-3366

Estover Road
Plymouth PL6 7PY
United Kingdom

Printed in the United States of America
British Library Cataloging in Publication Information Available

Library of Congress Control Number: 2007936271
ISBN-13: 978-0-7618-3904-0 (clothbound : alk. paper)
ISBN-10: 0-7618-3904-6 (clothbound : alk. paper)
ISBN-13: 978-0-7618-3895-1 (paperback : alk. paper)
ISBN-10: 0-7618-3895-3 (paperback : alk. paper)

™ The paper used in this publication meets the minimum requirements of American National Standard for Information Sciences—Permanence of Paper for Printed Library Materials, ANSI Z39.48—1984

Dedication

I write these memoirs at the urging of my family and friends. I am not certain what they had in mind—perhaps to inspire their children and preserve a sense of the family for the next generation or to describe a life lived at the center of history. Perhaps, in the telling, some of it has been accomplished.

These memiors are dedicated to those who have meant so much to me in my life:

> To Gene Eisner, without whose skill, understanding and compassion I would never have had a life to write about; and
>
> To my beloved family who has given me the love I learned to appreciate as the most important glue that binds us together as a family and, by extension, as human beings.

Contents

Acknowledgments

Among the many people whose interest and encouragement were a continual inspiration and prod to write these memoirs, there are several who made very special contributions:

Dr. Natalie Naylor, Professor Emeritus, Hofstra University, whose fascination with exploring the history of my Aunt Rosalie immeasurably enriched my understanding of her;

My editors and agent who started out as strangers and ended up as enthusiastic allies and friends;

Bette Lee Hanson, my editor, who is responsible for the absence of what she called my "psychobabble" as well as my treatises on regulatory agencies, the consumer movement and Betty Freidan's *Feminine Mystique* that I had prepared originally. The book is the better for her sensitive editing and for making the whole enterprise a fun experience;

Donald Brown, editorial advisor, who was a fount of all wisdom in bringing these memoirs to life; and

Patricia E. Moody CMC, my agent, without whose enthusiasm for the project and indefatigable research on potential readership, these memoirs might never have seen the light of day.

June 2007

Introduction

I CHOSE THE TITLE OF MY MEMOIRS TO CAPTURE THE STRUGGLE I HAVE had throughout my life to integrate my goal of self-fulfillment with my search for full humanity. *Tearing Down Walls* expresses my struggle to be the person I hoped to be as well as the efforts it took to enter the profession I had chosen for myself. I have tried to articulate my drive to be accepted and underscore the many personal and professional rejections—both real and imagined—I received and internalized. I hope that these memoirs show my lifelong effort to integrate my emotional and professional lives that for too long were strangers to each other.

This is the story of how my life evolved in a world of work that was profoundly anti-women, when women graduates were urged to seek work as secretaries and women lawyers were seen as an aberration. But, above all, it is the story of why I sought out psychological help and how, through psychoanalysis, I found meaning, identification and liberation as a woman.

We are, of course, products of our parents, our parents' parents and the world we live in. About three years into analysis I had an epiphany. I realized that what had happened to me as a child was not irrevocable. In the end I was the master of my soul; I had the power to decide how to shape my life and perhaps, most importantly, I learned I could integrate my rich family history into what I learned about myself and do it without losing my struggle for true humanity and concern for those less fortunate. And especially, I learned to love and trust the younger generations in my family who came to mean so much to me in my life, especially as I grew older.

As I look back, my life is also the story of my developing concerns for the "little people," as my family so disparagingly called them who did not share their lifestyle or historical family background. It documents my growing empathy and understanding for those who were denied the opportunities I had, and who continued to be discriminated against regardless of their accomplishments. This is my story as honestly as I am able to tell it.

My "Mayflower" Family

I was raised in a family of privilege and social standing that dated its ancestry to before the American Revolution. They regarded themselves part of an American aristocracy that entitled them to privileges that were denied to those less fortunate. In addition to an entrenched belief in the family's superiority, there was an unbreakable code of behavior that determined who you were and what you were supposed to become. I resented it and rebelled.

I always knew I was unwanted. I recall my mother telling me when I was very young that after I was born she took immediate steps to ensure such an "accident" would never happen again! My birth was such a disappointment that my father went on a three-day drinking binge after learning he had yet another daughter and not his dreamed-of son and namesake. My two older sisters had already carved out their turf with my parents. Ann, the first born, was clearly my mother's favorite and Betty, the second, was the chosen favorite of my father. I was the favorite of our governess, Anne M. Elbs. Fraulein, as we always called her, came to us from Germany when I was six months old and provided all the love I remember as a young child.

I grew up in this emotional vacuum, determined to resist conforming to my family's social expectations that a woman's only role in life was as wife and mother. I eventually managed to develop a well-rounded life outside their expectations and did achieve a respected professional career. But through it all, I was haunted by a deep emotional turmoil I could not articulate and that prevented me from expressing myself. It wasn't until I had gone into psychoanalysis that I was able to develop as a person, and resolve the inner conflict between who I was and what my mother expected me to be. For good or ill, my family was a powerful influence on me.

I never had any illusions that mine was a happy family, or that my mother loved my father. It was a marriage of convenience entered into between two well-connected families to produce children—ideally, a male heir—that could carry on the family legacy. My mother's marriage to my father in 1910 was largely one of social convenience fueled by my grandmother's fear that her only daughter was fast approaching an age when she might become a spinster.

My family's ancestors came to America in the early 1600s and settled in New York State. Mother's family were DePeysters, Livingstons and Petits from Scotland, Holland and France, who settled along the Hudson River and in the newly colonized Dutch city of New Amsterdam (New York City). The DePeysters were largely landed gentry preoccupied with their lands in New York's Hudson Valley. The Livingstons, on the other hand, were active in New York politics and represented the interests of the landed gentry. They opposed the dominance of the Anglican church and later the establishment of an Anglican college in New York. They also supported military action against the French in Canada over the opposition of the mercantile interests who feared the disruption of trade that might result. Mother's paternal family, the Shorts, were primarily professionals: scholars, lawyers and physicians who lived in New England.

William Livingston founded a political journal dedicated in part to "correcting the taste and improving the Minds of our fellow citizens." At the time of the Boston Tea Party, it was a Livingston who despite fears of mob rule, pushed hard for a ban on the importation of tea in the colony. The Livingstons were strong patriots and active in both the first and second Continental Congress. They remained active in business throughout this period and in the 1800s became the target of more populist minded citizens who fought against those who monopolized various elements of commerce in New York.

The Shorts were socially prominent in New York City and the Jones were regarded as landed gentry from Long Island, and although the two families viewed each other with a degree of disdain, father was socially acceptable. The marriage spared mother the disgrace of spinsterhood and enabled father to fulfill his hope of having a son and namesake.

They agreed to begin their lives together alternating summers on Long Island with winters in New York City.

My mother, Anna L. Short, had been sent away to Switzerland to recuperate from the tuberculosis she had contracted shortly after the death of her adored father, Edward Livingston Short. From all reports, he was a gentle man who died young from Bright's disease when she was only sixteen. Her brother, Livingston, was the first to notice she was hemorrhaging and immediately, after the diagnosis, she was sent with a governess to a Swiss sanatorium for treatment and convalescence. This interrupted her high school education at the Brearley School in New York City and she never did graduate. I believe she always regretted it. Mother was a bright woman but a product of her times when social etiquette and grace were considered more important virtues than education.

Apparently, mother's TB went into remission shortly after she arrived in Switzerland and in youthful high spirits she would evade her governess and proceed to have a wonderful time in St. Moritz where the sanitarium was located. We grew up hearing stories about her popularity and especially how an Englishman had fallen in love with her and wanted her to marry him. But my grandmother, Anna Livingston Petit Short, was a demanding matriarch and would have none of it. She would not allow her daughter to marry a stray Englishman in the British Army. That stray Englishman, incidentally, went on to an illustrious army career as British Field Marshall Bernard Montgomery who helped lead the Allies to victory in World War II. So much for family snobbery!

Grandmother Short demanded that her daughter return to New York and begin the process of making the appropriate social contacts. Mother met my father, Charles Herbert Jones[1], at one of the many social functions young girls attended in those days as they began the search for a husband. Father had been left profoundly deaf after a bout of meningitis when he was eighteen and could engage in conversations only with the help of a hearing aid. But he was one of the few remaining eligible bachelors in New York society.

My grandmother also kept a tight rein on her only son, Livingston. Both he and my mother grew up in New York City in the family house on East 37th street. My beloved Uncle Livy was bright and, true to custom, was sent away to prep school. He later graduated from Williams

College and Columbia Law School and, as a devoted son, lived with his mother until her death in 1923. Livy had a highly successful business career as president of General Motors Acceptance Corporation and during World War II directed the Lend Lease program in North Africa.

I had heard a lot about Livy's business colleagues and met several of them on the yachting outings he invited the family to attend. But I knew little about Livy as president of GMAC. According to a biographical note in the book by Dunbar Maury Hendricks, *We Met By The Way,* "Livingston Lyman Short was to the manor born—in truth as well as in the way he conducted himself throughout his life. He loved luxury. He spent wisely and got his money's worth. He was something of a showman in the process of being boss, friend and mentor."

Hendricks, who worked for Livy, also wrote that Livy set high standards. "He molded each of his key men, bringing out their strong points and character, their talents and their attention to those unwritten laws which before the bloodbath in Europe left the state all but bereft of standards and those who tried living up to them."

Livy took early retirement in the 1950s, and was immediately sought after as an ambassador. But this was at the height of Senator Joseph McCarthy's anti-communist witch hunt, and Livy, who was homosexual, could never have passed the security check. So he turned these offers down. I feel it was a tragic loss for the country. Instead, Livy spent the last years of his life traveling and dividing his time between his homes in Long Island, New York City, and Palm Beach.

My father's ancestors were Joneses and Gardiners. They came from Wales and England in the early 1600s and helped settle the British colony of Long Island. The original settler was Lion Gardiner, who was born in Scotland, and along with his Dutch wife arrived in the new world in 1635. He was an engineer and held a contract from the crown to build an armed fortress at the mouth of the Connecticut River.[2] They lived at Fort Saybrook where Lion was named chief commander and where he spent a good deal of his time protecting the settlers from the Indians.

According to written reports, Lion Gardiner managed to be friendly with many of the local Indian tribes and intervened on their behalf when there was trouble.[3] Robert Payne, the Gardiner family's biographer, said Lion's attitude towards the Indians was complex; "He feared them, detested them, loved them and liked playing tricks on them." [4]

Payne also recounted that Wyandance, who was chief of the Montaukeetes Indians, approached Lion and wanted to make a deal that would permit Wyandance to trade with the fort. Lion agreed but on one condition: Wyandance would have to prevent the Pequot Indians from attacking Gardiner's ships as they sailed into Montauk Point from the fort. They struck a binding deal. When Lion retired as commander in 1639 he moved his family to Machanaake, the small star-shaped island off Montauk Point.

Originally, Lion had received a land grant to parts of the island from the Earl of Stirling, Secretary of State for the Scottish Kingdom, and he managed to expand his land by purchasing some of Chief Wyandance's island holdings for ten bolts of trading cloth.

When the chief died in 1659, he willed Lion his remaining island holdings in gratitude for the help and valuable counsel Lion had given him and his son during their long years of association. When Lion died six years later, he was described by his biographer as "one of the very few Englishmen who was aware that there was any tragedy at all in fighting in the swamp and forests against the Indians." [5] From that time on, Machanaake has been known as Gardiner's Island and had remained in the hands of a Gardiner until August 2004, when my cousin Bobbie died at the age of ninety-three. Bobbie was the last Gardiner to bear the family name and with all due pretension had declared himself 16th Lord of the Manor. [6]

In my childhood memory, Gardiner's Island was a glorious place filled with infinite mystery and great stories. Perhaps the most famous centered on Captain William Kidd. It was rumored that Kidd left some of his treasure buried on the island. He was not the pirate of mythology, but rather a substantial citizen of the new American state who owned a large house in New York City and was described as a "happily married man, a British sea captain and a pew holder of Trinity Church."

The British Crown had given Kidd orders to capture as many privateers as he could and return them to England for punishment. After one particularly long voyage around the Cape of Good Hope, Kidd captured an Arabic sailing ship that was carrying a great Mogul's daughter and her substantial dowry of gold and silver to an arranged marriage with the Sultan of Madagascar. Kidd conquered the vessel and proudly sailed it into New York harbor. Only then did he learn he had been declared an outlaw by the British government. [7]

While Kidd fought to clear himself of this charge he was sheltered on the eastern end of Long Island and was defended by his lawyer, Robert Livingston, one of my mother's ancestors. Livingston had invested in Kidd's trip from England and had gone on to Boston to defend him. According to the story, Kidd reportedly sent an emissary to John Gardiner and requested to hide some of his treasure on Gardiner's Island before he sailed on to Boston to defend himself. Gardiner agreed but Kidd never did return to claim it. He was imprisoned and eventually sent back to England where he was hung on the gallows.[8] Kidd died maintaining his innocence and claimed he left the bulk of his captured treasure at Hispaniola (Santa Domingo) before he sailed for New York. His story was never believed and only a small portion of the gold and silver was ever located on Gardiner's Island. The bulk of the treasure has never been found.[9]

Another Gardiner story concerns Julia, a direct descendent of John Gardiner. She is reported to have been a great beauty who was carefully schooled in the social etiquette of her day. Along with her family, she spent a season in Washington in order to participate in the social life of the nation's capital.

During the course of the many Washington balls she attended, she caught the eye of the new President, John Tyler, who had just succeeded to office after the unexpected death of William Henry Harrison. Tyler, a widower for six months and thirty years Julia's senior, confided to a friend that he was smitten with her beauty and immediately began to court her. They married in 1844 and Julia threw herself into the politics of the day. She actively supported her husband in his efforts to admit Texas into the Union.[10] One year later, James Polk defeated Tyler in his bid for reelection and the couple moved to the Tyler plantation in Virginia where Julia presented her husband with seven children.

When the Civil War broke out, the northern and southern branches of the Gardiner family split. The northern Gardiners were strong anti-slavery unionists while Julia and the Tylers were equally active in supporting the Confederate cause.

When John Tyler died in 1872, Julia lived on as his widow for twenty-five years and is reported to have visited the White House often. During one of those visits Julia asked President Andrew Johnson why there were no portraits of presidents' wives in the White House. President

Johnson suggested she should send her portrait and promised to have it hung next to her husband's.[11] She promptly complied and thus began the tradition of hanging the portraits of America's first ladies in the White house alongside those of their husbands.

The Jones family saga is equally colorful.[12] Major Thomas Jones was described as "a protestant gentleman of Strabene, Ireland," but it appears he was also a privateer.[13] His grandson preferred to declare he was "engaged in numerous expeditions under letters of marquee." He was of Welsh extraction and came to Oyster Bay from Jamaica about 1692. He married Freelove Thompson, who also owned large properties around the Bay. Being the shrewd man that he was, not only did he enlarge his own holdings through marriage, but he also purchased land from the Indians so that at the time of his death he had an estate well over 6000 acres.

During the American Revolution, the Gardiners, DePeysters and Livingstons had no trouble supporting the movement for independence. The Joneses were a different story. They believed that autonomy of the British colonies could be achieved by staying within the British Empire using political agitation rather than revolution to force a change of British policy in the colonies. [14]

In June of 1776, Major Thomas Jones was arrested "upon a charge of refusing to obey a summons of the Committee of New York Provincial Congress" and was ordered to show due cause why he should be considered a friend of the Americans. So, as a prisoner of the American Army, he was sent to Connecticut and released only after he signed a promise not to give aid and comfort to the enemy.

Thomas Jones's name was included in the Act of Attainder (a legislative declaration of treason) passed in New York in October of 1779. He was arrested and his major land holdings were confiscated. In 1780-81, he was released and with his wife and niece, sailed to England to go to the hot springs of Bath for his health. He always intended to return to America when the Bill of Attainder was repealed but he died in 1792 before he could return. He was buried in Stratham, England, where his widow had his tombstone inscribed, "By strangers found and by strangers mourned." [15]

A part of the major's property on the south shore of Long Island became known as Jones Beach State Park. Robert Moses, the famous New

York City parks commissioner and a friend of my father, gave it that name. Moses purchased the land from the Long Island townships of Oyster Bay and Hempstead, but we don't know how this property came into the hands of these townships. One theory is that Thomas Jones had given the land to the state for a bird sanctuary; another is that it may have come into the state's hands through the original Bill of Attainder that was placed on Jones' property during the American Revolution.

Whatever the story, what I find important is that Jones property has been used to serve an important public purpose. It has provided New Yorkers and Long Islanders with a pristine beachfront park of 2400 acres with room for egrets, ibises and black skimmers. I am proud that my father played a role in suggesting to Moses that he set aside parts of Jones Beach to be used by residents of the various Long Island communities and New York City.

The early Joneses were active in politics and business. Samuel Jones played a key role at the New York state convention that led to the state's adoption of the Constitution. The Joneses were also Chancellors of New York and in the 1800s were active in the whaling business. They established the Atlantic Mutual Insurance Company to support their whaling business and they participated in extending the Long Island Railroad to the Huntington area. These various business enterprises were referred to as Jones Industries.[16]

Interestingly, the writer James Fennimore Cooper was married to a Jones family member, and he wrote: "The Jones family has now furnished legislators and jurists to the colony and the State for more than a century."[17] The writer of the Introduction to Major Thomas Jones' *History of New York* said: "It is the only family, it is believed, not only in New York but in America, which under the British and the American governments has from the beginning of its existence in America, from generation to generation, continuously preserved and maintained its prominence in political life and high public opinion." [18]

Unfortunately, the family wasn't able to sustain these accolades for long.

The Jones and Gardiner families were joined in 1838 when Elizabeth Gardiner married Charles Hewlett Jones. Their daughter, my grandmother, Mary E. Jones, married her first cousin, Dr. Oliver Livingston Jones, in 1873[19] and through this union solidified their land holdings on

Long Island. Mary E., as she was always called, was father's mother and another matriarch who dominated the lives of her family and refused to allow her physician husband to practice his profession! When we were growing up there were models of the veins in the human hands stored in the carriage house on the Long Island property that I always assumed belonged to my grandfather. Later in life, when he was living in their house in New York City, he committed suicide. No explanation was ever given about why he took his life but there was mental illness in the family and two of his sons suffered from the disease.

There were six children from this marriage: Louise, the oldest, never married and lived next door to us in Cold Spring Harbor; then there was my father, Charles; next was Rosalie, a lawyer, author and suffragist; followed by Oliver, who never married, suffered from mental illness and died very young; the fifth child, Arthur, did marry but was also mentally ill; and the youngest was Philip, who died in the flu epidemic of 1918.

My domineering grandmother believed that no Jones should work and that they must only buy land, not sell it. "We do not believe in letting our lands lie idle," she is quoted as saying, "whether they are along the desert seacoast or on crowded Manhattan. It requires continual watching and industry to keep them all improving and not to allow any of them to deteriorate in value."[20] Her children seemed to have gotten the first message but not the second. With the exception of Rosalie, none of them tried to make their land productive and both Louise and my father lost much of their land to the state because of their failure to pay back real estate taxes.

This was the family I was born into on December 10, 1920. I was baptized Mary after my paternal grandmother, Mary E. Jones, and was given the middle name, Gardiner, to reflect that side of the family. I grew up feeling like the family's ugly duckling, overshadowed by my two attractive older sisters, and I developed a deep sense of inadequacy. I struggled within this dynamic until I found success in school. It was my opportunity to achieve and it fulfilled my need for recognition even as I coped with a growing and debilitating anxiety.

Mine was a privileged family with long historical roots but with values I didn't share. For the sheer sake of survival, I tried desperately to hold my own against their authoritarian view of society and whenever I would challenge their values they would throw at me the admonition, "Don't be like your Aunt Rosalie."

Notes

1. The family name was Hewlett not Herbert, but the Joneses and the Hewletts were fighting at the time my father was born so they preserved the "H" but named him Herbert.

2. All of the material on the Gardiner family is drawn from Robert Payne, *The Island* (Harcourt Brace, 1958), p. 43. The late Robert David Lion Gardiner, the last Gardiner who bore the family name, gave Payne full access to the Gardiner papers. Gardiner died in 2004.

3. Payne, *op.cit.,* p.43.

4. *Ibid.*, pp. 85-88.

5. *Ibid.*, p. 95.

6. *Ibid.*, p. 54-55.

7. *Ibid.*, p. 145-46.

8. *Ibid.*, p. 147.

9. *Ibid.*, pp. 145-46.

10. *Ibid.*, p. 221.

11. *Ibid.*, p. 226.

12. Most of the material on the early Jones family was drawn from the three-volume *History of New York*, written by Major Thomas Jones, grandson of the original settler, Thomas Jones.

13. Jones, Thomas, *History of New York: The Revolutionary War*, (New York, Historical Society, 1879), p. liii.

14. As Major Thomas Jones wrote: "There can be no greater error than to suppose that the loyalists as a whole were willing to submit quietly to the exactions of the mother country, and her invasions of their rights and liberties as English subjects. As Americans they felt these grievances, and were as indignant at the treatment they were subjected to, as those of their countrymen who took up arms. But they wished to fight the battle for those rights and liberties and the redress of those grievances with the powerful weapons which the constitution of England gave to them as to other Englishmen—weapons which had proved successful before, as they have proved successful since, in similar emergencies, freedom of speech, freedom of the pen, freedom of the press. They desired by political agitation to force the home Government to a change of policy or to drive it from power and place in office the foes of the oppression of the colonies."

15. *Ibid.*, p. lxv.

16. *Ibid.*, p. 44.

17. John H. Jones, *op.cit.*, p. 14.

18. *Ibid.*, p. lxxiii.

19. John H. Jones, *op.cit.*, pp. 144 and 177.

20. *The New York Press*, Section 2, June 21, 1908.

Aunt Rosalie, the Maverick

Rosalie Gardiner Jones paid little or no attention to social convention despite having been presented to the Queen of England. She chose to be a contrarian, which probably led to her success, as well as to her eccentricity.

When I was growing up, Rosalie and my aunt Louise lived across the road from us in Cold Spring Harbor in the large, fifty-room mansion built by my grandparents. I can vividly remember her piercing blue eyes and the brown wig she wore simply because it was easier than trying to keep her hair under control. To me, Aunt Rosalie always appeared to be hostile and antagonistic toward the entire family and there were always family fights between father and his sisters. I never knew exactly what the fights were about. All I remember is that for some reason Aunt Rosalie thought my sisters and I were siding with father against her and perhaps it was easier for her to blame everything on us children.

Rosalie was born in 1883, the middle child in a family of six. Unlike her three brothers and her sister, she was the only one to graduate from college.[1] She went to Adelphi College in Brooklyn and later was the first woman to graduate from the Washington D.C. College of Law. She also received a Master's Degree from George Washington University in 1919 and followed that with a Doctor of Civil Law from American University in 1922 where she published her doctoral thesis, *The American Standard of Living and World Cooperation*.[2] She was brilliant and was not afraid of expressing new and forward thinking ideas.[3]

Yet despite these impressive credentials and because she was a woman, Rosalie was never able to practice law in Washington D.C. Instead, she was forced to volunteer at the District Courthouse and occasionally would have cases assigned to her. I remember her story of the young forger she represented who taught her everything there was to know about forgery law. She asked him why he kept going back to forgery and he said it was a good way to earn a living. Furthermore, he said, he spent more time outside jail than in!

But Rosalie's real claim to fame was as a suffragist. From 1911 through 1913 she immersed herself in the push for voting rights for women, a movement that followed a long feminist tradition dating back to Abigail Adams.

The early nineteenth century suffragists also were abolitionists, but the male organizers of the anti-slavery movement barred them from attending or speaking at their conventions. They also had taken up the cause of temperance and once again faced a constant struggle against the tide of male resistance. Traditionally, the movement had concerned itself with respectability. They held their meetings in members' parlors where they would educate women about politics and teach them how to participate in conventions dealing with abolition and the temperance issues.

By the beginning of the twentieth century, the movement had become stale and sedentary with a split between those who were willing to work with men and those who were not. When Rosalie joined them in 1911, the split was in full force. In 1912 she was elected president of the Nassau County branch of the National American Women's Suffrage Association and in direct opposition to many of her fellow members, she took a strong stand opposing purging men from their ranks

Rosalie had a rare gift for public relations. She is credited with breathing new life into the movement. One of her earliest acts of defiance was to urge her members to participate in an outdoor suffrage demonstration—a very radical idea at the time. She kept the issue of "Votes for Women" in the media's eye, and set about to publicize the cause not only in Long Island and New York, but throughout the country.

In 1911, when she and her fellow suffragists demonstrated on Wall Street, they were met with a shower of eggs and tomatoes. But Rosalie remained undaunted. In 1912, sitting in a wagon painted suffragette yellow and drawn by a horse named Suffragette, Rosalie toured 250 miles of rural Long Island in a "Votes for Women" campaign. When she spoke on Main Street in the small Long Island town of Northport, she drew a crowd of 200 before going on to a similar horse and wagon campaign in Ohio.

By December 1912, she had organized and led the first "Voting Rights for Women" march to the New York state capital in Albany. But the group was overcome by bad weather. It was bitter cold and the marchers were beset by snow as they stopped to greet the townspeople in their attempt to convert them to the cause.

Their eventual goal was to meet with the legislators that were due to convene at the state capitol on January 1, 1913. Their plan was to present petitions to Governor William Sulzer, who had promised financial support for women's rights. This was welcome news to Rosalie, who up until this time had been paying all expenses of the campaign out of her own pocket. Unfortunately, only five of the original suffragists made it to Albany. However, when they did arrive on the Capitol steps on December 28 they were accompanied by a large number of citizens ringing bells and blowing whistles, along with a scattered number of the new motorcars eagerly honking their horns.

It was at this event that Rosalie and her original band of 200 stalwart marchers gained national fame. The press from Florida to California covered them extensively and Rosalie was given the title "General Jones."[4] Her PR instincts were so clever that she delighted in the doggerel that appeared in the Lincoln, Nebraska *Journal*: "Now the hike along the Hudson seemed a foolish trip and vain. But it gave them advertising from Los Angeles to Maine."

My grandmother was furious with Rosalie. Mary E. was an active opponent of the suffragist movement and a supporting member of the New York State Anti-Suffrage Association. She told a *Brooklyn Eagle* reporter, "The idea (of marching to Albany) is ridiculous. They will be exposing themselves to the snow, wind and ice and are jeopardizing their health. It is absolutely foolish."

But Rosalie was undaunted! She acted on what she believed despite her strong-willed mother.

By the end of 1912, spurred on by the fame and success of her Albany march, Rosalie was busy organizing the famous march to Washington D.C. and drew up plans to present a similar petition to president-elect, Woodrow Wilson. On February 19, 1913, carrying yellow knapsacks, staffs and "Votes for Women" buttons, General Jones and 300 marchers began the trek from Newark, New Jersey to the nation's capital. Although many of the original marchers dropped out along the way, the organizers continued to pick up local suffragists on their 240-mile trek.

The march was plagued with problems from the beginning. Marchers were frequently denied access to hotels and food. They were yelled at, jeered from the sidelines and more often than not were given the wrong directions about the proper route that caused the marchers to go miles out of their way. By the time the group arrived in Baltimore, many had dropped out or decided to ride part of the way in the automobiles of friends. But not Rosalie. She was one of the stalwarts, the self-styled "Old Guard' that insisted on walking every step of the way from New York. And there were others who had joined them from Philadelphia and Baltimore.

When the group finally arrived in Washington DC, another roadblock was thrown their way. They were informed that only women who had marched from Newark would be permitted to march into the city. Rosalie stood her ground and adamantly proclaimed: "the men of my party and the newspaper men and women who have plodded along with us will march with our 'army' in the entry into the National Capital or General Jones and her colleagues will not enter Washington." That settled the argument.[5]

But Rosalie was not so successful in resolving the problem her army faced from the demands of Negro suffragists who intended to join the march. Rosalie's army had been warned in Wilmington, Delaware that as they approached Maryland, they would be forced to take a positive stand on their demands.

As the army approached Winans, Maryland, the warning came true. They were met by a large band of Negro women carrying their own yellow banners, "Votes for Negro Women." Although the white suffragists ignored them, the Negro group marched along behind them for a short distance and then retired.

As the group reached Laurel, Maryland, once again they were approached by three carriage loads of "colored" women wearing "Votes for Women" badges. Again their tactics were to follow the army, cheering and making it appear they were participating in the suffrage demonstration.

Rosalie was forced to take a stand. She refused to let them join the army and told the press, "An army of Negro suffragists will join our army? Well I guess they will not." Her lieutenant, "Colonel" Ida Crofts, took the same position and said, unequivocally, "If the Negroes attempt to march with us into Washington, then I will not." [6]

I have no idea if Rosalie was prejudiced and refused to see the Negro suffragists as a part of the movement or whether, as I would like to think, she was unwilling to let the march on Washington be bogged down by adding Washington's southern racism into the mix. Above all, Rosalie was a pragmatist. In addition to the race issue, the march was beset with disagreements about strategy, but loyalty to their general kept the army together. A few words and a smile from General Jones kept everyone in good spirits. The *Washington Post* reported: "General Jones is not a general in name only. Like Julius Caesar, she knows how to deal with discontent, ambition and jealousy among her centurions." [7]

As a result, defections from the march were kept to a minimum.

One of the goals of the suffragists was to participate in the inaugural parade and then present a letter to President Wilson. The idea of presenting the letter was abandoned when the president declared in advance he would refuse to receive such a delegation. However, the group did manage successfully to join the inaugural parade.[8] Rosalie's group joined the other white suffragist sections of the parade and together they numbered over 5000 women. The parade was divided into seven different sections. The college section alone included over a 1000 women. There were also sections representing labor, business, social workers, writers, and a variety of professional women. Several of the suffragist floats included in the parade also demonstrated the worldwide scope of the movement for woman's suffrage.

The women had to fight their way foot-by-foot up Pennsylvania Avenue and they were only able to complete the march after cavalry troops from nearby Fort Myer were sent in to protect them. The press reported: "No inauguration has ever produced such scenes, which in many instances amounted to little less than riots." [9]

Nevertheless, the very jeering and heckling that made it almost impossible for the 5000 marchers to fight their way through the mob helped them gain national attention and sympathy for their cause.[10]

After the march, Rosalie returned to Long Island and continued to work for the movement. She organized a series of pageants and parades on Staten Island, as well as in various towns on Long Island and in

New York state. She also daringly flew over Staten Island in a two-seater Wright biplane to toss out a handful of yellow leaflets boldly titled "Votes-for-Women." The headline in the *New York Times* read: "General Rosalie Jones Flies for Suffrage."

Never idle and despite her family's privilege, Rosalie continued to defy tradition. Between marches and tours, she trained herself as a mechanic and ran an automobile repair shop. As Rosalie explained it, "it is because of my adherence to the cause that I am going into business." She prophesied that after the vote was won, "the women who will be of value will be those who are trained, not the helpless dependent ones incapable of looking after their own property without the aid of men."

She chose the automobile repair business because automobile repair was regarded as man's work and she foresaw the time when women would be driving themselves and needed to know how to deal with their cars. She also held farsighted ideas about the role of women in society and was never loath to express them: "I believe," she said, "that every one should work, married or single. If a married man does not want his wife to work for a salary, he should see that she receives an equal percentage of his salary ... Industry has made it possible for ... women to enter business in subordinate roles. They should not be content to stop there." [11]

It took five years and more activism before the 19th Amendment was passed giving women the right to vote. Rosalie was living in Washington when the amendment was finally ratified by enough states to be signed into law on August 18, 1920. She had returned to the nation's capital to begin her graduate education while she continued her advocacy work for women's rights. As a political activist, she campaigned for the Progressive Party's candidate, advocated for better treatment of labor and other social reforms and became active in the Women's International Peace movement.

It was in the course of this work that she and several colleagues visited the Capitol to lobby the senator from Washington, Clarence C. Dill. They felt his support was essential because he was unalterably opposed to its goals. In typical fashion, Rosalie and her colleagues felt that made him the one they should meet. After being kept waiting for an hour, they were finally admitted into Dill's office. "One would think that we were book agents," Rosalie is reported to have told the senator. His response was equally direct: "I prefer book agents to many women lobbyists."

In dramatic fashion, this meeting produced a fervent four-year courtship of Rosalie by Clarence Dill and they married March 15, 1927 at St John's Episcopal Church in Cold Spring Harbor. The marriage attracted a lot of publicity. According to the *Washington Post,* "It is always a fillip to the interest of the people on the sidelines when a woman who has scorned the pretensions and claims of the 'stronger sex,' and a man who has been a bit of woman hater in his way, fall in love."

Senator Dill, meanwhile, was quoted in the press explaining his attraction to Rosalie: "I am not a Victorian, believing all women should remain in the home. I have met women political leaders for whose mental attainments I had and still have the sincerest respect. But never until Miss Jones bawled me out for thwarting her committee had I met a woman who, for me, combined charm and political acumen. Even angry as she was, she showed a keenness of intellect that won my admiration, as it would have won the admiration of any thinking man. Her mind, keen as it was, remained distinctly feminine, and full of the charm of femininity. I may add its unexpectedness. She thought of more things to argue about in fifteen minutes in my office and more ways of calling me a dodo, in a nice way, than a male political opponent would have conceived in a couple of days." [12]

Rosalie, meanwhile, was described as "pretty, financially independent and politically minded." She strongly believed she was sufficient onto herself, and men were seen as interruptions and distractions. [13]

When Rosalie agreed to marry Dill she insisted that the word "obey" be struck from the marriage ceremony. "It is not a word a self-respecting woman of this century likes to give a man", she said. "Mutual understanding, affection and consideration govern the relations of husbands and wives. So long as love and honor are there, the word obey won't be needed. And if we should stop loving each other, the word wouldn't mean anything."

She also refused to be given away at the altar. "I'm solely responsible for what I am doing," she said, "Nobody can give me away. I'm independent and my own boss. How ridiculous for a brother or somebody to hand me over to my new lord and master like a woman of the harem. I'll give myself away." I clearly remember going to Aunt Rosalie's wedding and seeing her stride down the aisle by herself wearing a red dress!

Five years later, in 1932, Franklin Delano Roosevelt was swept into office in the midst of a major Depression. Suffrage was a reality and Rosalie had what to all accounts was a successful marriage to a United States senator. She was elected president of the Congressional Wives Club and was invited to give speeches around the area. On several occasions, along with other senators' wives, she had tea with Eleanor Roosevelt.

But, tragically for her, the marriage did not last. According to Senator Dill, Rosalie did not keep up her end of the social duties that were expected of a senator's wife. Perhaps it was predictable and undoubtedly there were other issues between them.

In 1936, the marriage ended in a messy divorce. Dill, among other things, accused her of burying their dogs in the back yard. Rosalie fought it all the way. When the marriage was over, Rosalie returned to the family home in Cold Spring Harbor and, on and off, lived with Louise in the red roofed stucco mansion that had been her home when she was growing up.

Rosalie's maverick ways continued when she took over Eton's Neck beach on the north shore of Long Island that was owned collectively by the Jones family. True to her fashion, she promptly invited lower income people from the neighborhood, some of them blacks, to build small shacks on the beach and then she collected ground rent from them. It's my understanding that Rosalie kept these rents and refused to share them with my close-knit family. Obviously, this was a constant source of irritation and perhaps the cause of many of the family arguments.

Despite her growing eccentricities, however, Rosalie's mind was always active. Without any training in either biology or animal husbandry she got interested in multiple births and proceeded to purchase a herd of goats to see if she could determine why so many of them had multiple births. I have no idea how she did this but I do know she would send her goats to graze in the South in the winter and then they would come back to Long Island in the summer.

During World War II, there was a serious shortage of oil. On one occasion, Rosalie's goats were returning from the South and the railroad car carrying her goats were put on a siding in order to accommodate the rail cars carrying desperately needed oil to the Northeast. Rosalie was notified of the action and immediately wired back her reply. Of course she understood the need, but if they wanted to offload her goats they must also understand that under the Interstate Commerce Act of 1887 they were required to milk all 150 of them. The goats arrived in Cold Spring Harbor the next day!

On occasion Rosalie tethered a few of her goats in an abandoned Jones house near Cold Spring Harbor. To stimulate breeding, she had tethered two of the goats together in the house and one jumped out the window and was strangled. The next day a headline appeared in the local paper, "Rosalie's goat commits suicide." Obviously she was not popular in the community.

Another resident of Cold Spring Harbor, a Mr. Guile, equally disliked by the neighbors, had dared to grow commercial dahlias on his property. This was not something you were supposed to do with land in that area. (As my grandmother Jones insisted, land was to be enjoyed, not commercialized.)

As could be predicted, one day Rosalie's goats ate Mr. Guile's dahlias. He sued Aunt Rosalie for damages, and the community, enjoying the spectacle, split over which side to root for. The case was tried in the Oyster Bay courthouse and was the longest trial the community had ever witnessed. Rosalie represented herself, of course, and she won the case because she dug out an old law of the range that still was in effect on Long Island. It held that property owners must fence in their property against any wild life in the area. Mr. Guile was ruled at fault and denied all damages.

Clearly, Aunt Rosalie was a many-faceted person. My sister Betty and I viewed her very differently. Betty remembered when she was a freshman in college, Aunt Rosalie came up to Wellesley bearing a copy of the *Iliad* that she had received as a child and wanted Betty to have when she entered college. Once, when Rosalie was in her nineties, Ann's oldest son, John, and I visited her in Brooklyn where she had been living with friends. I remember her being a little foggy but her eyes still flashed when she harked back almost immediately to her suffragist days. I remember her wagging her finger at me and saying, "you can't do it without the men, Mary."

Unfortunately, when I was young, Rosalie was mainly the object of the family's scorn. However, as an adult I have great empathy for my Aunt Rosalie and only wish I had known her better. She was a brilliant woman born too soon. She was a woman more comfortable in opposition than in winning. And I can only imagine how difficult it must have been for her to have a domineering mother like Mary E. Jones, who was against all the things she believed in: women's rights, the peace movement, and a wide range of other social issues. Still, despite society's dictates, and sometimes against insurmountable odds, Rosalie managed to be herself and made important contributions to the cause of women.

Rosalie lived for many years with her sister, Louise, and in later years divided her time between Cold Spring Harbor and Brooklyn, New York where she lived with the Maxwells, some friends who clearly appreciated her as a person and cared for her until she died at the age of ninety-two. She is buried in the family cemetery behind St. John's Church in Cold Spring Harbor, in front of the family mausoleum. The mausoleum had been vandalized in the 1940s and my father's bones had been scattered, so our family had it bricked up. Rosalie's headstone, true to form, stands by itself outside the mausoleum site.

Growing up when both she and Aunt Louise were around was one of my more vivid reminders of the Jones family legacy.

Notes

1. My father attended Yale College but he discovered his deafness made it impossible for him to do the work. There were no aides for deaf people in educational institutions in those days.
2. Jones, Rosalie, *The American Standard of Living and World Cooperation*, (The Cornhill Publishing Company, 1923)
3. Jane Matthews, "General" Rosalie Jones, Long Island Suffragist, *Nassau County Historical Society Journal*, 47 (1992): presents a comprehensive description of Rosalie's life, p. 27.
4. *Washington Post*, February 27, 1913
5. *Washington Post*, February 27, 1913
6. *Washington Post*, February 27, 1913
7. *Ibid.*
8. *Washington Post*, March 2, 4, 1913
9. *Washington Post*, March 4, 1913
10. "Feminism In the Repair Garage", *Newsday*, 1913
11. *Washington Post*, April 24, 1927
12. *Ibid.*
13. *Washington Post*, April 24, 1927

Growing Up a Jones

My sisters and I spent our summers in Cold Spring Harbor where the Jones family had been living since the early 1700s Every year, from May to September, we lived a leisurely country life just thirty miles from our apartment in New York City.

The house we lived in was originally the gardener's cottage that was built in 1783. When my grandparents were alive their gardener lived there until they had to move into it in 1909 because the main house had burned down. They lived there for a few years while a new fifty-room stucco mansion was being built on the adjoining property. My parents then moved into the cottage in the early years of their marriage. They added a wing that included a butler's pantry, an expanded pantry, four additional upstairs bedrooms (two for the maids and two for us and our governess) plus a den downstairs where my father played solitaire by the hour. But most of the rooms were small and built to preserve the heat so typical of those early colonial New England homes. They called their new home Jones Manor. Lotti Saida, the Polish farmer and an expert groom, lived in one of the other smaller cottages on the estate. He and his family had lived next door to my parents when they first got married and, at my parents suggestion, moved with them to Jones Manor to take care of the estate. In addition to the horses that Lotti groomed, we had cows, chickens and a wonderful vegetable garden. Mrs. Lotti (the only name we knew to call her) took care of the chickens and also would make delicious homemade pot cheese, that to my recollection far surpassed the commercial cottage cheese we buy today.

Several other buildings were scattered around the property: an empty icehouse, a blacksmith shop where a blacksmith would come to shoe our riding horses, a wooden building that my father used as his office that still had his initials carved on the door, plus an old carriage house that we used as a garage, that still contained a few of the family carriages. My parents had a playhouse built for the three of us as it was unthinkable that we should ever want to spend a summer anywhere else!

My father's sister, Louise, lived alone in her parents' fifty-room mansion except for a cook, a paid companion, and Rosalie, who moved in and out from time to time. I think Aunt Louise occasionally leased out some of her fields to some Polish potato farmers in the neighborhood, but she refused to rent to any farmer who intended to take advantage of President Roosevelt's farm policy that would pay farmers for not growing potatoes. She viewed it as a socialist giveaway program.

But for the most part, like the rest of the Joneses, Louise only gazed at her land, and true to her mother's dictates never did sell any of it. Late in her life, after she had smashed up her car, she would walk to the village and adamantly refused any favors from us even though we lived next door. At the time of her death, she had only her cook as companion and was living in only one room in that huge fifty-room house. But she still owned the original 125 acres she had inherited from her mother.

Living on Long Island, I was surrounded by the legacy of the Joneses. St John's Episcopal, where we went to church, had been built by my great grandfather John Jones and other relatives in 1836. Inside were plaques dedicated to the many Joneses, including father, who had been vestrymen over the years. There was also a family cemetery in the woods behind the church where my grandparents and my father were buried in the family mausoleum.

My most vivid memories of the family are their constant fights over property. My grandmother, using one of the best law firms in New York City, had drawn up the most complicated will possible in order to set up a variety of different trusts to make certain the property stayed in the family as long as possible. These trusts were a source of many family quarrels. I had always heard that there were more lawsuits in the Mineola Courthouse involving the Joneses than any other family in the county.

Every weekday father went into New York to the real estate office he maintained at 90 Wall Street with his sisters, Louise and Rosalie. As far as I know, they did very little business but remained true to the dictate of their mother never to sell any Jones property. Presumably they managed the property they owned in New York City and collected rents. I always heard that father mostly played double solitaire with the office secretary, Helen McCabe.

When the Depression hit the country, father didn't have enough cash to pay the interest on the mortgages for property he owned on Sixth Avenue in New York City. In an effort to save the holdings, he went to my mother and her brother, Livingston, begging them to lend him the money. They refused to bail him out, so these city lots were foreclosed. Despite my mother's lifelong quarrels with my father over money, she never acknowledged that she could probably be living in clover had she or Livy been willing to save his New York City property.

Throughout his life, my father, like his sister Louise, held tenaciously to his mother's principles of never selling property. As a result, when he died, most of the 125 acres of the property he had inherited had already gone to the State for back taxes. The only property left that he could not sell was the sixteen acres held in trust for his children.

Actually, I don't remember mother ever showing much affection for my father until very late in her life. To her, marriage was the thing to do and it created the secure base that allowed her to function. She never did understand any other option. She always told us that early in her marriage she had to make a choice of whether she would devote her life to her children or to herself. She chose herself. Uncle Livy traveled a lot and every summer she went with him to Europe.

She hired Anne M. Elbs as our governess, who had emigrated to this country from Germany when she was in her early twenties just before the United States entered World War I. Ours was only the second family in the states she worked for and very quickly she became a family fixture. With Fraulein, mother felt she had hired a good governess and therefore was doing what was best for us. She also saw to it that we went to the best private school, had skating lessons, made proper social contacts and, later, when we were older, went to the right dances and had the inevitable coming-out party.

Our upbringing was modeled on that of the British upper class; seen but not heard, cared for by a governess, told what was good for us and expected to obey. The three of us were dressed alike and I hated it. What was a suitable dress for my sister, Ann, five years older than I, was hardly suitable for me. I remember with horror a dress we had to wear—gray crepe de chine with a red velvet collar. I yearned for a frilly pink party dress and black patent leather shoes! In sum, we lived a very traditional life, summering in the country and spending our winters in the city. In those days very few of the "socially acceptable" families lived in the country all year long.

Mother was direct and controlling. She wanted me to do all the things she thought were socially important and never understood that maybe I had different aspirations and was developing different social values. And my father had his own set of biases; old families like ours shouldn't mingle with "ordinary people." His mother and father were first cousins. Apparently neither of them could find anyone else they believed appropriate to marry so they settled for each other. But interestingly, father never shared any of my mother's social ideas about bringing up children. He wanted us to live in Cold Spring Harbor all year long and attend the local public school. Many of the Joneses had gone to public school, and his taxes supported them, so he argued we ought to attend them. My mother would have none of that.

Neither father nor his opinions counted for much within the family. He was deaf, passive and went on alcoholic binges that kept him away from the family for days at a time. These would be followed by weeks of recovery while Fraulein watched over him to make sure he didn't get out and buy more liquor. As children, we were told when we went out with him to make sure not to let him get a drink. Also when he was recovering from one of his binges we would be taken into his bedroom and paraded in front of him—all in an attempt to shame him into not drinking. It left me with a terrible feeling of disgust. My sister, Betty, more compassionate and caring than I, hated the idea of shaming him that way. I don't know how much his alcoholism affected us but for years I was a teetotaler and my two sisters both married men who drank heavily. Yet we never talked about our father's alcoholism.

It must have been depressing and very difficult for my deaf father to be surrounded by my mother, three boisterous children and Fraulein. He would retreat to his den, isolate himself, and play solitaire by the hour! I remember him getting violent only once. We were in the country when he took his shotgun from his den into the dining room and threatened mother and Fraulein. I don't remember what this issue was about. Fraulein threw a large silver bell at him and while he was distracted she took away his gun. Betty and I were in the den trying frantically to telephone Uncle Livy, who lived nearby, to ask him to come over. I was about four at the time and insisted on doing the dialing. I have learned since how angry Betty was that I was always trying to take charge, even at four!

Even though my sisters and I didn't know our father very well, he obviously had qualities that endeared him to his friends. One of his close friends was Dr. Samuel Riddle, a geneticist at the famous Cold Spring Harbor Biological Laboratory that sat on land given by the Jones family. He also was a friend of Robert Moses, the architect of Jones Beach and La Guardia Airport.

LaGuardia was built on land that also had belonged to the Joneses. My father probably got to know Moses when he was negotiating to buy the family property for the airport. Father always maintained that LaGuardia Airport, as it was planned, was not big enough to accommodate future air traffic; and due to the neighboring wetlands was likely to sink—two accurate predictions that to this day are plaguing the planners. Also, when Moses was conceiving of Jones Beach, it was my father who suggested he set aside parts of the beach complex for the residents of Long Island townships of Oyster Bay and Huntington on the north shore, and Babylon on the south.

All of this was in direct contrast to the father I knew. I only remember his railing against taxes, zoning (he thought you should buy the view not zone against people obstructing it) and his children going out in "twosomes." In his day, he'd say, young people went out in groups to house parties. My father couldn't accept that times had changed even though he could foresee the future of La Guardia Airport and Jones Beach.

Uncle Livy was the only male in my family whom I looked up to—blond, handsome, strong and obviously a dedicated and hardworking executive. Livy was a great opera lover and maintained the same subscription at the Metropolitan opera that his mother had before him. She left him four seats on the aisle, midway in the orchestra section. But Livy had the habit of falling asleep in the second act and snoring. So he purchased additional seats in the first row on the left side of the orchestra next to the bass section, hoping it would drown out the whistle and snorts of his naps. The front row seats also had another advantage. They were strategically placed near the side exit so that he and his guests could sneak out for a drink at a little bar across the street if he felt the opera got tedious.

I was only six when he took me to my first opera. I used to be invited a lot, particularly when the Met was playing Wagner and the other operas that were not popular with the rest of my family. I volunteered to go, because I wanted so much to be included. But when I would accompany him I didn't think the base fiddles were very successful in drowning him out and even as a little girl I was torn between letting him snore or waking him up, which he did with an enormous snort.

All of this had a wonderful consequence for me. I have been an opera fan ever since and have continued to maintain the same mid-orchestra seats that were my grandmother's. I also started buying classical records at a very early age and clearly remember my first records: Musetta's waltz from *La Boheme*; Wagner's *Rienzi* Overture; Tchaikovsky's Fifth symphony and, of course, Beethoven's Fifth. I was only fourteen when I used my allowance to buy my first stand-alone record player. It was a Magnavox and I loved it. Music was an important emotional outlet for me then and has continued to this day.

Livy knew how to enjoy himself. He loved his yacht, the *Stella Polaris,* and used it to entertain his friends and business colleagues, to commute between his home in Oyster Bay, Long Island and his office in New York City, or to visit friends along the Long Island Sound. He took it on frequent cruises to Maine, Canada or Block Island. Typically, his car would accompany the yacht along the shore so Livy could get on and off as he pleased. Several times I was invited to go along and it made me feel very special.

Livy's swimming and fishing were notorious. He would appear on the deck of the *Stella,* take one plunge into the Sound, then re-emerge as Roget, his valet, held a towel in one hand and a martini in the other. His fishing was equally catered to. He held the rod in his hand while he dozed. If he got a bite, he gave a sigh of impatience, pulled the fish in and then gave the line to Roget, who took the fish off, replaced the bait and Livy resumed his fishing! And here was I, his young niece, dying to get a bite but never succeeding.

But my adored Uncle Livy was a homosexual who often used mother as his hostess and cover. It was a discreet arrangement that served them well. She spent her summers traveling with Livy in Europe and, after my father died, spent the winters being his hostess in Palm Beach. There they were part of the social ambiance at the formal dinner parties so typical of that environment.

I was very naive as a young person and didn't recognize Livy's homosexuality until much later in my life. I do remember some of the young men whom he befriended from time to time, but never thought much about them until law school, when I became close friends with a fellow law school student whom Livy had introduced me to. When the young man proposed to me, I was my usual hesitant self. It was at this point that Livy fixed me with his eyes and told me that if I ever planned to marry the man, I must talk to him first! I wasn't ready to get married so it was never an issue. But years later, I realized that Livy might have come out of the closet in order to protect me from my own naiveté.

Fraulein was the other major influence in my life. I am convinced she was responsible for holding the family together. I can't remember Fraulein ever taking a vacation. She also began to do all the cooking and housework after my mother decided in the 1930s to let the cook and maid go as her way to save money during the Depression.

Mother was always talking about saving money; strangely we believed we were poor despite the opulence that surrounded us. Fraulein also nursed my father when he would return home after an alcoholic binge and she would play backgammon with him in the evenings. Of course we were too busy to bother and my mother was always off doing something else.

Fraulein's influence was quixotic. My strong social conscience probably came from her. I knew I was her favorite. But I was also very jealous of Ann and Fraulein didn't help that situation. She would point out to both Betty and me how much my mother favored Ann. Fraulein was very authoritarian and in many ways insensitive to children's needs. I remember vividly when I was about twelve giving her a present for Christmas. She promptly took it back to the store because it wasn't practical. I stood outside the store in tears because she didn't like what I had so carefully picked out. Yet she was the one who came to my school events and made sure our birthdays and Christmas were properly celebrated.

But she, like my mother, based her actions on "what was good for us " rather than exploring what we might want or need.

Our lease on our fourteen-room apartment on Park Avenue expired in 1933, and we moved into a seven-room apartment on Fifth Avenue, in the same building where Uncle Livy lived. Also that following summer my mother decided we were too poor to open our house in Cold Spring Harbor, so she rented it. Father, with no say in the matter, was shipped off to spend the summer with his sister, Louise.

Mother took Betty and Ann to live with her and Uncle Livy in Oyster Bay and I went with Fraulein to Germany to spend the summer with her family in Ulm. I had a wonderful time. I managed to learn German very quickly as I played with Fraulein's nieces and nephews. Hitler was just beginning his rise to power and I can remember when his Nazi storm troopers stood in front of the few Jewish owned stores in Ulm pressuring shoppers not to go inside. I also vividly remember a Nazi parade in Stuttgart where we were visiting some of Fraulein's family. Fraulein and I stood silent with our arms by our sides while her sister and family joined the crowd yelling "Sieg Heil" Sieg Heil." I don't think I understood very much of what it all meant but Fraulein was very clear in her feelings about this rabble-rousing Austrian leader. For me, it all blurred.

It was a glorious summer. Becoming fairly fluent in German, I enjoyed the excursions we made to the countryside and the evenings in the garden cafes. But these halcyon days quickly disappeared into the darkness that was Hitler Germany. It was 1947 before I went back to Germany and visited Fraulein's family. Her mother and father (Grossmutter and Grossvater to me) had died; a nephew had been lost in Russia but her sisters and brothers made it through the war.

A brief hiatus took place in Fraulein's life with us. It came after father died. Mother had met an old boy friend, Rod Wellman, whom she called Honey, and the two of them spent a weekend at the Guernsey Inn at Montauk Point, on the eastern tip of Long Island. Fraulein was incensed, packed up, and left. She worked with two other families on the Island and did not return until after Honey died, rather unexpectedly. Fraulein then moved back in with mother and stayed with her in her New York apartment.

When mother would go to Palm Beach every winter, Fraulein stayed with her sister in a small walk-up apartment in the city. After Livy died she began to accompany mother to Palm Beach and died there in 1970. Fraulein is buried in our family plot in Cold Spring Harbor, near my mother, Uncle Livy, my sister Ann, her second husband, Robert Crooker, and her daughter, Abby, plus the headstone for my father whose bones had been scattered after the vault had been vandalized.

I was always uncomfortable with the privileged life we led and distressed over the falseness of my family's values. They felt superior to everyone who did not come from an "old family." We had servants, two homes, and money for private schools and skating lessons—all things my mother thought were socially important. She was not interested in what we wanted or liked and always thought we weren't sufficiently appreciative of what she gave us. I wanted to go away to summer camp but to her that was ridiculous when we had such a "lovely country home." So, between the dictates of Fraulein and mother there was very little tolerance for being myself, whatever that meant.

Also, I was always acutely aware of how much we had compared to others. When many of the truck farms on Long Island were sold off to developers and houses began to spring up, I thought it was wonderful. I liked the idea of less affluent families sharing the land my family had enjoyed for so long. When my family railed against President Franklin Roosevelt's policy of raising taxes, I secretly cheered. Many blacks lived in New York City and I used to see them on the bus I took going back and forth to my music lessons and I was acutely aware of how they lived. I recoiled when my family was so contemptuous and called them "Niggers." [1]

Ann, Betty and I went to the Nightingale Bamford School, a small private school on 92nd Street in New York City. It was a "socially acceptable school" but gave me a very good education. As a little girl I remember being embarrassed because mother wouldn't pay the extra fee for milk and crackers that were handed out at recess. This made me stand apart from my classmates. I also have the vague recollection that we were not permitted to buy summer uniforms because they were expensive, so we were forced to wear scratchy, hot woolen winter uniforms all year long.

But I loved my classes. They were very academic and I excelled, plus school gave me a life apart from my family. I was active in glee club, the drama club and played piano in the orchestra. I didn't realize that I had achieved such proficiency on the piano but my diary notes that I played not only for orchestra but for other school events as well. I went religiously to my music lessons that I had started on my own. Mother wasn't particularly interested in my playing so I paid for them out of my allowance. Then, a little conscious-stricken, she upped my allowance to cover my expenses. But my mother wasn't overjoyed with my practicing. Often when I started to play, doors would slam and my mother would call out, "Do you have to practice now?"

Sports were also a major outlet. We had two wonderful gym teachers whom my friends and I were forever taking out to tea. We also played a lot of ping-pong with some of the teachers and even with the formidable Miss Maya Bamford, the school principal. She was able to reduce most of us to tears in a matter of minutes if we were sent down to her office for discipline. I had a small group of friends and we visited back and forth in each other's homes and went a lot to double feature movies. In my sophomore year, I began to get into trouble in school. Nothing serious, mostly giggling in class, being disruptive, playing practical jokes and doing things that were regarded as inappropriate. Miss Bamford threatened to suspend me. But by my junior year, I grew up and by my senior year I was elected president of the student body.

Through it all, I was very tied to my family. In my diary I talked about visits to mother's Aunt Emily and her husband, Bob. They were the ones who took me to concerts at Carnegie Hall for the first time. We also had a wonderful Cousin Tillie on my mother's side of the family who was a great flamboyant soul, highly rouged, dyed hair and painted blood red fingernails. She was very real, had no pretensions and was a great deal of fun to be around. I remember her saying to us, quite seriously, how the dark meat of the chicken was so much more nutritious than the white and then promptly helping herself to a large portion of the white!

I also recall when I was growing up that mother had what she used to refer to as choking attacks. She was afraid to go out by herself and Fraulein had to accompany her as she went running to her doctor to get Vitamin B shots. Fortunately for her, doctors then were available and willing to see their patients at almost any time.

When I was about fourteen, my mother became concerned because I appeared sad and depressed much of the time. She took me to her doctor who knew nothing about children's traumas or depression and who dismissed it all as part of growing up, so it was promptly ignored. I don't remember her being concerned again until after I had graduated from college when I was in my first job and getting constant intestinal cramps. Once again she carted me off to doctors and once again they found nothing. The possibility that I might be having emotional problems never occurred to any of us.

Despite being freer during my adolescent years, I was always fretting about my authoritarian family. At the end of my junior year in high school, I remember asking mother if she would object if, when I got out of college, I took an apartment rather than living at home. That started a row. According to my diary entry at the time, she ranted on about how she had given up everything for her children because she felt it was her duty. I responded by asking her if it had been any pleasure and she replied, "No." Then I note in that same entry: "We were very annoyed at one another. Mother couldn't understand that I might want to be independent." What fascinates me about this diary entry is my clear recollection that she had told us very early that she had chosen to live her own life rather than devoting it to her children.

Perhaps because she wasn't able to finish high school due to her tuberculosis, mother did believe in a college education. She agreed to pay for my undergraduate education but when I decided to go to law school I had to pay for it myself. My mother's sense of obligation to her children did not extend to graduate school and she strongly disapproved of my seeking a professional career. The proper role for a woman was to get married.

Summer was a very busy time throughout my teen years. We had horses, and my sisters and I would ride to our hearts content. I shared my father's love of riding and prized those few moments we could be together. I recall one weekend staying out in the country with him and trying to cook the meals—hardly my specialty—but I was game to try. Even with those prized shared times with him I can't remember him as a loving father who cherished his daughters. Instead, he seemed overwhelmed by all the women around him. I remember one Sunday dinner when he stalked out of the dining room muttering "women, women, women!"

My parents loved fox hunting and I learned to love the sport when I was quite young. Indeed, I think it was the only activity I ever saw them enjoy doing together. The meets began in the early fall and would take place at the various stables near us. I always felt uncomfortable because my family would never pay the hunting fees for me. They felt since the hunt frequently rode over our property, it was not necessary to pay for me. Once I remember the hunt coming up our front drive when I had had no warning. I think I was about ten. I jumped out of bed, saddled up my gray pony and tore after them as fast as my stubborn little pony would go. Later, as I grew older, I rode father's horse, Sister, a sixteen hand red roan. In the fall she and I would go to the meet around 6 a.m., trembling from the cold and relishing all the excitement. She was a wonderful horse. I was very near-sighted and didn't wear glasses when I was riding but I could always rely on Sister not to take a jump if it wasn't safe.

In some ways these were idyllic days. I would visit with my girl and boy friends, and in the winter we went to the formal, highly social New York dances. Although my lasting memory of these dances was one of horror and fear of being stuck (not cut in on), I record in my diary only that I went and had fun. I also went to the proms at my various boy friends' prep schools but worried constantly over whether some boy did or did not like me.

In the summer we played tennis, attended sports events and played a lot of bridge. But our major activity was sailing at the Seawanhaka Yacht Club. The sailboats were made available to Junior Yacht Club members and we could use them any time. I loved sailing. It gave me a great sense of independence knowing we could sail whenever we felt like it. Every summer, at the end of the season, the owners of the big sailing ships made their yachts available to the members of the Junior Yacht Club and we would crew those wonderful schooners—twelve-meter sailing ships or sloops—for an entire weekend. It was a glorious experience!

Summers also meant I could visit my best friend, Priscilla Buckley, in her home in Sharon, Connecticut. I loved visiting the Buckley family because we were free to do whatever we wanted. And I remember Priscilla's younger bother, Bill, later of *National Review* fame, as a chubby little boy of six playing the *Minuet in G.* Bill still plays the piano, as well as the harpsichord. Aloise, Priscilla's older sister, was a live wire and would think up all kinds of tricks to play. Plus, she was old enough to drive so we could drive all over the area.

The Buckleys also had a wonderful Capehart automatic record player that could be heard throughout the house. Priscilla and I would sit and read and listen to it by the hour. Priscilla's parents were not around very much but they, like us, had governesses and a wonderful music teacher who joined in on all our tricks. They were a happy family and I enjoyed being with them. They had a gaiety my family lacked.

Also while I was still in high school, I received my first marriage proposal from a young man who was the youngest and only boy in a family of six older sisters! He would come to the Seawanhaka Yacht Club dances driven by the chauffeur in the family limousine. I am afraid we weren't very nice to him. However, he must have taken a fancy to me and he proposed one night while we were at a dance. I was aghast. I couldn't believe any one would want to marry me so I instantly decided he must be crazy.

Ten years later, after law school, when I was living in New York, he called me up and told me he had seen me on the street. I was flabbergasted that anyone would recognize me after so long a time. Around this time I also received two other marriage proposals but I would always tell my boy friends we were too young and really didn't know what love was. I always found it disconcerting when they would return some years later, introduce me to their fiancée and agree I was right about not having been really in love!

This seemingly carefree childhood came to an end when I went away to college.

Notes

1. Yet much to my horror, when I was rereading my diaries, written when I was about sixteen, I found myself once making a reference to "Jews and niggers" just as my family did. It is hard for me to understand that, as my conscious recollections of the many battles I had about that kind of prejudice are so contrary.

Away from Home at Last

I was one of only four of my class of sixteen at the Nightingale Bamford School who went on to college. Fortunately, my mother believed we should get a college education and saw it as a way for us to support ourselves, if necessary. But she also believed with equal fervor that after college, marriage was the only acceptable option for a girl.

Ann didn't go to college. She was the youngest in her class and as a result didn't do very well academically. Instead, she dutifully followed my mother's dictates, married at twenty-one and had her first child the following year.

Betty set a different pattern. She excelled in school, and with the encouragement of her science teacher enrolled at Wellesley where she majored in English literature. Betty was the example I chose to follow.

I suspect part of mother's positive feelings about education were a direct outgrowth of her own experience, and never finishing high school. I believe that was a lifelong regret. She was a very bright woman who, shortly after returning from Europe, was offered a job in the trust department of the Central Hanover Bank in New York City. She had been handling her father's estate work with the bank so they knew her. Someone in the bank was obviously farsighted enough to realize that increasingly women would be dealing with the bank and it would be in their self-interest to have a woman on the inside who could stimulate new business and deal with woman clients. Unfortunately once again her mother interfered and would not hear of her daughter working!

To the day she died, mother never held a job or volunteered for anything. Volunteering wasn't done very much in her social circle, with an exception made during World War II. Wartime was considered different, so she worked with Traveler's Aid at New York's Pennsylvania Station, greeting and helping soldiers as they were passing through. She enjoyed it, even though it meant getting up at 6:00 am. But after the war she did what was considered socially acceptable and returned to her life of bridge, parties and traveling.

Getting into college was not difficult for me. I took a college aptitude test and a few college boards but I didn't start seriously looking at schools or thinking much about them until my senior year at Nightingale Bamford. Betty was just finishing her sophomore year at Wellesley, so it was natural for me to apply there. My good friend, Priscilla Buckley, had a sister who had gone to Smith so I was also mildly interested in that college. In addition to Smith and Wellesley only two other schools were considered socially acceptable: Vassar and Bryn Mawr. It never crossed my mind and certainly not mother's, to think about a coeducational college. No one in my high school class considered such an option, since that meant going to a state university. Also, confronting sororities and the social life they entailed never appealed to me. I was, after all, a product of my sheltered and very narrow environment.

So I applied to Smith and Wellesley. Smith turned me down saying I was not college material; why I don't know. Wellesley was either less discriminating or, as I prefer to believe, more perceptive of my potential! In any event they accepted me and I happily enrolled in the fall of 1939. Mother, father and Fraulein drove me up. I was excited but also a little anxious.

I had been assigned to Noanette, one of the freshman houses in the village of Wellesley. There was very little difference between houses other than their size. We were about 40 girls in Noanette and I wanted a single room because I had spent my entire life sharing a room with either Betty or Fraulein. So I certainly wasn't going to ask for a roommate now that I was finally free.

The rooms were small with a single bed, a desk, a bookcase, a wardrobe and a chair. So even with a room to myself I had trouble finding enough space for my phonograph and all my records. We all made our own beds and most of the girls sent their laundry home to their families. It never had occurred to me to do that and certainly my family would have had a fit. So I did my own in the washing machines the college provided and loved the independence and being away from home at last.

Miss Wiggins was the housemother at Noanette and looked exactly how a Miss Wiggins ought to look: hair pulled back tightly in a severe knot at the nape of her neck and always dressed in somber clothes. In those days there was a strict curfew rule about going out at nights or on weekends. We had to sign out and Miss Wiggins saw to it that the rules were carefully followed. Other than that we had very little contact with her and I don't believe it occurred to any of us to question the system.

College was an eye-opener for me. Wellesley was basically a middle-of-the-road school that catered to middle class, middle income and mid western girls. For the first time, I met girls from different parts of the country. Some had gone to private schools but most had attended public schools. Many of their fathers sold insurance or worked in manufacturing jobs. This validated for me my long held conviction that my family was different but not special and that there were other people in this world without my particular family background who were educated, artistic and had made a good life for themselves in a variety of jobs. But what I loved most about college was the freedom it gave me to be myself and the exciting intellectual world it opened up for me.

I liked many of the girls in my house and became part of a group who stayed together most of the year. My friends soon disabused me of most of the strange notions I had grown up with, the most glaring of which was that we were poor. They all hooted at that and I realized how much I had bought into my family's notions. We had a special category for the "drips," girls we didn't like. Toward the end of my first year I was sitting at a table with some of them and remember being fascinated listening to them talk about fellow students in the house they regarded as drips! That taught me an important lesson.

My closest friend was Mary Gilmore, or Gil as I called her. At one point early in our friendship I was put out about something she did (I don't remember what) and I didn't talk to her for almost a week. We had a good laugh when we finally discovered she hadn't even noticed. About the time of my birthday Gil got a letter from mother informing her that she was sending up a birthday cake and that Gil was to arrange a birthday party for me. The letter was signed Anna L. Jones. From that time on Gil always referred to my mother as Anna L.

We took most of our meals in our "vil" house and bicycled about a half-mile to the collage campus,. Even though Betty and I lived in different houses, we often went to the "vil" together and it was wonderful for me having my sister in college when I got there. It certainly helped ease my transition into a new, strange and exciting environment.

Except for the required science courses, I loved my classes and very early gravitated towards history and political science that had always been my favorite subjects in school. I had several wonderful history professors who made me realize I was right to choose that subject as my major.

In my freshman year it was Gwendolyn Carter, a professor of European history. She conveyed an exciting sense of historic realities, not by some boring recitation of battle dates and revolutions but as a vibrant tapestry of how people lived their lives in previous centuries. She gave me a sense of excitement about history, and listening to her teach awakened in me the joy of learning. Professor Carter had polio when she was only four and ever since was forced to walk with crutches. I found it extraordinary that she was oblivious to them. I became very friendly with her and would go down to the house she shared with another history professor, Louise Holborn, and clip newspaper articles for them. We talked about everything—about their lives, what was going on in the world and about the fascinating discipline of history. I began to come alive intellectually. I also learned from them how to be frugal. I watched them as they stacked their dishes in the dishwasher until it was full or they ran out of dishes and only then would they run the dishwasher. It's a habit I follow to this day.

In my sophomore year, my history professor was Elizabeth Hodder, who taught a course in British Tudor and Stuart history. I can visualize her now standing in front of the classroom, striding back and forth while reciting passages from the Pym ship money case. I can't remember now what the Pym case was about but I do remember how excited I was by her vivid description of this historical period in English history.

Seal Thompson, who taught Bible, was another teacher who fascinated me. At the time it was a required course for this Congregational college and one of the most stimulating courses I took in my four years at Wellesley. I can still remember her intoning passages from the Old Testament; all five feet of her, ramrod straight and always dressed the same, in an ankle length green cord dress. She vividly brought to life for me the ancient struggle of the Israelites as they defined their relationship to God.

Very early in my college career I decided I wanted to teach. In both my sophomore and junior years, I took several education courses from Isabelle Stephens, who insisted we call her by her first name. Isabelle lived in Cambridge which added a different dimension to the college environment because most of my professors were single and lived in Wellesley. Her classes were stimulating and to this day I credit them with teaching me how to think. We read books like *The Education of Henry Adams* and then spent several classes defining and differentiating between "freedom from ... " and "freedom to.... " Her classes were an exacting intellectual exercise. Part of our assigned homework was to keep a journal of our thoughts and observations on life. One day I realized that I had turned in my journal with a disastrous bridge score written on the back page of the notebook. When the journal came back the note, "poor we," was written next to the terrible bridge score. That defined Isabelle for me. She was interested in us as human beings not just as students in her class.

In general, I was happy at Wellesley. I studied hard and life was busy. I went to classes, to the library, to the "vil" for coffee with other college friends, and I played a fair amount of bridge. But unfortunately, starting in my freshman year, I was often depressed. I would have severe mood swings and started having difficulties with my friends. I would feel left out or jealous and had the sense they took friendship more casually than I did. This made it difficult for me to relate to them. Sometimes I would be with my friends and suddenly start to shake uncontrollably. Eventually it would pass and I didn't think any more about it. It was many years later when it began to happen again that I sought professional help.

I certainly was not a loner but somehow I always felt apart and different. I have never liked to work under pressure, so I would finish studying for exams early and then the night before exams would go to the movies, a habit that drove my friends crazy. They also said they envied me because I knew what I wanted to do when I graduated.

Most of my friends hadn't made up their minds about what they wanted to do but most expected to get jobs and then get married. That was also my plan but in my mind that didn't conflict with my having a meaningful career. But I was by no means alone in my quest. In our class of 407, we had several artists, published authors, teachers, a Metropolitan Opera singer, five lawyers, one physician, one Doctor of Ministry, two MBAs and sixty-five with other advanced degrees.[1] An impressive list.

I was different only because I never married. There were only twenty-two of us who remained single. My sense of being different persisted for many years whenever I attended my various class reunions. I found the early reunions difficult because almost everyone came back with their husbands and talked endlessly about children and family. I had little to contribute. My classmates always made much of my achievements and it seemed very genuine. Nevertheless I felt the differences and a little removed. At later reunions, when my classmates talked about their grandchildren, I was able to talk about my wonderful nieces and nephews. And now at more recent reunions, even the grandchildren are behind us. We talk about our newest career—retirement!

I dated very little in college. Some of my old high school boy friends would come around when I was a freshman, but after World War II began most of them went off into the service. After Pearl Harbor the draft was in full effect and dating opportunities at an all girls' school were limited. I went once to a dance at an army base near Wellesley but found myself too anxious to really enjoy it. There were a few opportunities to go on blind dates, of course, but I didn't do that very much either. I can't remember why, I just wasn't particularly interested. I wonder now if my friends realized this and didn't suggest many blind dates to me.

But there were many exciting events I enjoyed at Wellesley. In my freshman year I heard Sergei Rachmaninoff in the Wellesley concert hall. It was a thrilling experience! But I remember being surprised by the lack of expression in his playing. I have no idea whether that was true or whether I was in one of my many mood swings and I projected that onto his playing. I also heard Ezio Pinza, the handsome Metropolitan opera bass, whom I had heard many times at the Met while I was growing up. He later became hugely popular for creating the romantic male lead in "South Pacific." Of course I went to Broadway to see it and loved it.

And there were many Wellesley traditions I found moving; step singing outside the chapel, for instance, and the beautiful ecumenical services where we would march into the chapel holding candles that gradually burned out as we took our places in the pews. Years later, when I was at the opera in the coliseum at Verona, Italy, the audience held lighted candles that burned out when the overture was over. It was thrilling and I became nostalgic thinking of that college experience.

After the war began, Eleanor Roosevelt came to speak at Wellesley and I was bowled over. Politically, I was a Roosevelt supporter but I had never particularly liked Eleanor. Her syndicated column, "My Day," seemed superficial to me and other than that, I knew little about her. But when she spoke at the college and recited her experiences talking to our soldiers on trains, on street corners or at local army bases, her deep compassion and love for them came through and she became one of my life long role models.

My father died in 1941, the spring of my sophomore year. He was 63. He had had an operation and developed pneumonia. They prescribed sulpha drugs. At the time it was the drug of choice for treating pneumonia, but he developed a severe allergic reaction. There was nothing they could do for him.

Betty and I were in New York during spring break when all this happened. We had visited him in the hospital and the night before his death had gone to hear *Parsifal* at the Metropolitan opera. We were not prepared for his death and were very upset, especially since this was the first death we had experienced in our immediate family. Mother arranged to bring his body to our house in Cold Spring Harbor and I remember being surprised by the number of local residents who came by to pay their last respects: trades people, farmers, and friends. Aunt Rosalie and Aunt Louise were still alive at the time and they were there with many other Jones relatives. After the visitation was over, we held a service in St. John's Episcopal Church and afterwards we all climbed up the relatively steep hill behind the church to reach the family cemetery where my father was buried in the Jones family mausoleum.

I went back to college, but found myself inordinately upset. I didn't really want to go home that summer. A close college friend of mine, Alice Cole, suggested I go with her to Colorado University's summer school. That seemed like fun since I had never been out West. It only remained for me to convince my mother who, to my surprise, agreed. I must have appeared more distressed than I thought. I don't remember what we studied in summer school but I do remember going on weekend outings, having evening campfire picnics and doing a lot of horseback riding. It was a welcome experience.

As the war progressed, there was a severe oil shortage and Wellesley made the decision in 1942 to close for the winter months. Many of us looked for jobs and I found one in a bank on Wall Street. I was assigned to the bank vault to clip coupons on the bonds owned by the bank's wealthy customers. I remember we weren't allowed to wear sweaters, a rule to keep us from slipping a bond under our shirts.

But I had problems entering the bank coupons accurately into the various accounts and then totaling them at the end of the day. The bank had a rule that no one could go home until all the accounts were balanced. After a while, the supervisors decided to check my accounts first, looking for errors and more often than not, they found them. But I kept my job.

I learned then that those of us who were in college and held only temporary jobs were earning more than the skilled high school girls who were permanently employed. I put on my Good Samaritan hat and spent a lot of my lunch hour trying to persuade these young girls not to settle for low-level jobs and urged them to go on to higher education. My naïve vision of going to college had no reality for them but they listened politely to my high-minded lecture. The next summer I shelved books in the bank's library and fortunately didn't have any of the bank's accounts to balance. But once again I continued my crusading lecture and once again it fell on deaf ears.

Also in 1942 in the middle of the war and my junior year, the Women's Auxiliary Voluntary Service (WAVES) was created and Wellesley's president, Mildred McAfee, was asked to set up and lead this new branch of the Navy. She took a leave of absence and appointed a triumvirate to run the college: the president of the Alumnae Association, the Dean of the college and one faculty member. I am certain this change in leadership had ramifications for the faculty and trustees, but as far as I remember, it made little difference to the students.

The war did bring about one change in my life that was pivotal. In my senior year, in addition to my regular classes, I and fifty or sixty other college seniors, were secretly recruited by the Navy to learn cryptography. No one was to know what we were doing and, as far as I know, it never got out until 2003 when a story about this super secret cryptography course was written up in the alumnae magazine.

I found the course difficult. I wasn't sure I would have been any good as a cryptographer, but circumstances dictated I would never find out. After we finished the course, I was preparing to sign the enlistment papers for the WAVES when it suddenly dawned on me I would be crazy to sign those papers with the problems I had with authority and my instinctive need to be a non-joiner and to feel free. I realized I could no more salute someone and say, "yes sir" than I could fly. So at the last minute I backed out. It was a critical decision and it turned me back to my first love, teaching.

In June 1943, I graduated from Wellesley and took a summer job at the Institute of Pacific Relations. I was to catalogue their map collections of Russia and East Asia and I had an interesting time. About a year or so later I asked them for a verification of my summer job, and I was mortified to learn no one remembered me. I had applied for a job at the Office of Strategic Services (OSS) and needed the employment verification for my security clearance. Fortunately, I got the clearance anyway so it turned out all right.

Wellesley had prepared me intellectually to face the world and after graduation I looked forward to the next step.

Notes

1. Wellesley College, Class of 1943 Fiftieth Anniversary Report, *1943-1993: A Half Century of Wellesley in the World.*

Judge Thomas Jones, Justice of the Supreme Court of the Province of New York, 1791. (from the *History of New York During the Revolutionary War,* by Thomas Jones).

Anne DeLancey Jones, 1791 (from the *History of New York During the Revolutionary War,* by Thomas Jones).

Samuel Jones, first comptroller of the State of New York. Called the "Father of the New York Bar." (from the *Documentary History of the State of New York*, vol. 4).

Charles H. Jones of Cold Spring Harbor, President of Queens County Agricultural Society, 1870.

Mary E. Jones, Mary's paternal grandmother, 1854.

Jones Manor House in Cold Spring Harbor, N.Y., home of paternal grandparents, Mary E. and Oliver Jones. The house burned down in 1917.

Home of Mary E. and Oliver Jones. Built after Jones Manor house burned down.

Louise Elizabeth Jones (Aunt Louise), born in 1875 and dressed for a costume ball, typical of the social parties for the New York gentry.

Photos: Newsday Archive & Huntington Historical Society

Rosalie and her "Votes For Women" wagon led by the horse "Suffragette."

Rosalie Gardiner Jones (Aunt Rosalie), in 1883, in the front row, fourth from left, leading her group of suffragettes on their march to Washington.

Rosalie Gardiner Jones (Aunt Rosalie) learning the business of automobile mechanics to prepare for women's future roles once suffrage was won.

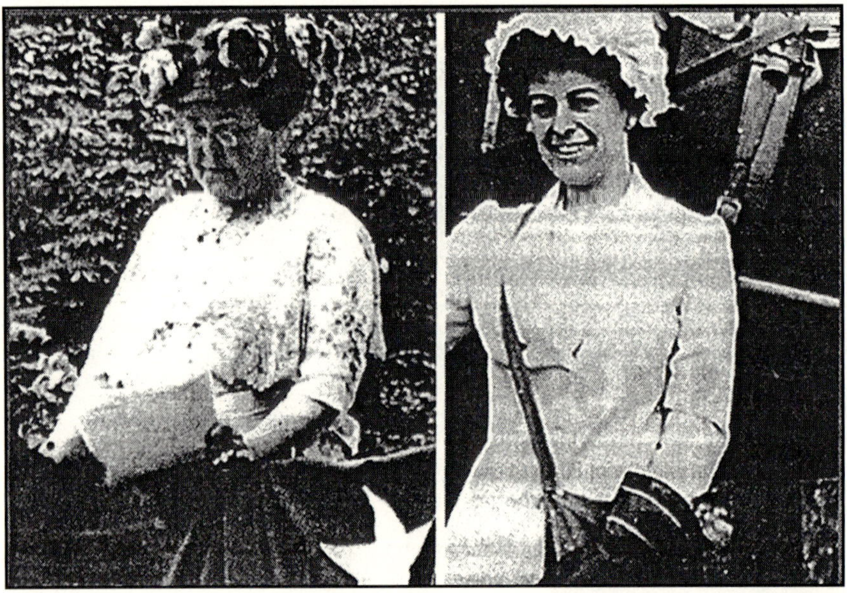

Alva Vanderbilt Belmont and Rosalie Gardiner Jones had more in common than unimaginable wealth and lofty social status. They also shared a passion for advancing the cause of women's rights. Together, with other suffragists, they haranged passersby in Manhattan together in 1911.

Rosalie Jones (left) and Ida Craft at the Women's Biennial Convention, in Chicago on June 11, 1914

Mary's grandfather, Edward Lyman Short, whose early death from Bright's Disease was so devastating to her mother.

Mary's grandmother, Anna Petit Short, another strong-willed matriarch among her ancestors.

Mary's mother, Anna L. Short at her wedding to Mary's father, Charles H. Jones in 1912.

Mary on her mother's lap with Betty (left), and Ann (right).

Mary and her mother's dog, Rip.

Mary's mother and father at their 25th wedding anniversary in their home, Jones Manor, 1937.

Father in his fox hunting outfit.

Jones Manor, built in 1790, where we lived every summer as children. Later renamed Hill House by my sister Ann after her family moved in.

Mary on her father's horse, Sister, riding to Hounds with the Meadowbrook hunt.

Fraulein, Anna M. Elbs, visiting Mary in her freshman year at Wellesley College.

Livingston Lyman Short, only son of Anna Petit Short, and Mary's beloved "Uncle Livy."

Mother and Uncle Livy together in Palm Beach where they spent their winters.

Fraulein with Mother in Palm Beach after Livy had died.

Teaching School, Joining the OSS

My last minute decision not to join the WAVES left me with no job after graduation. The war was in full swing and the country was on a wartime footing; food and gas were rationed and most of my boy friends had either volunteered or were drafted into service. Some of my Wellesley classmates had joined the WAVES, many got married and others had taken jobs in a variety of different businesses.

Although I had rejected the WAVES, I still wanted to be of service. I had always wanted to teach ever since I entered college although by this time most of the good teaching jobs had already been snapped up. Fortunately, Wellesley's career office found me an internship in history at the George School, a small coeducational Quaker boarding school in Newtown, Pennsylvania.

When I arrived at the school in September of 1943, I was scared to death and wondered what I had gotten myself into. Fortunately the principal, Richard McFeeley, was very welcoming, as was Walter Mohr, the much admired history teacher who was chair of the department where I was going to work. The school taught the seventh through the twelfth grades with small classes of about fifteen or sixteen held in a variety of stone houses dotting the campus. The students seemed to love the atmosphere, and to my eyes coeducation appeared to work very well.

I found the other faculty members all loved teaching and were highly intellectual. They also had deeply committed Quaker values they put into daily practice. This was true not only of the faculty but of the students and support staff as well, whether they were Quaker or not.

During the first few months I became friendly with the art teacher, a Japanese-American who had come to the George School after Pearl Harbor. She had been living with her family in Seattle, Washington when the Quakers rescued her from going into the internment camps created by our government for the Japanese Americans who lived on the West coast. They brought her to Philadelphia, found a place for her to live and then got her a job at the George School. We became good friends. She left the George School after the war and went to New York to work as a decorator at Altman's. When the Korean War broke out Altman's put her in a job that did not require her to be on the main sales floor. After the Korean War was over, however, they put her back on the floor dealing with customers!

I also became friendly with a most imaginative teacher, John Macintyre. He had come to the George School from a small public school in a low-income community in Lower Marion, Pennsylvania. John believed strongly in starting where the students were, in his Lower Merion school he used comic books as a tool to encourage his students to read. I had always believed engaging students in their own learning was the way to teach and I credit this view in part to the challenging education courses I had taken at Wellesley. And here was John actually doing this.

I was assigned to teach an eighth grade European history class that consisted of middle-range students who were not expected to go to college. I started out in the traditional way—teaching the history of Europe in chronological order. But when I got to the Industrial Revolution I thought it was time to switch gears and look at history in a way that might have more meaning to the world my students knew. I hoped they could identify with the American labor movement of the 1930's and from there get interested in other times and other countries where the labor movement got its start. We hadn't proceeded very far when I noticed that my slower students were coming to life.

My brighter students, however, came to me and said, "Miss Jones, when are we going back to studying history?" Perhaps I hadn't made the connection of the labor movement to the Industrial Revolution clear enough, or perhaps, as I think, they were too trapped in the traditional way of viewing the world chronologically.

As I look back on that experience now, it reminds me of the summer of 1947 when I took a break from law school and enrolled in a summer school at the University of Zurich in Switzerland. While I was there, Heidelberg University announced the opening of a two-week session for German and foreign students and I jumped at the chance. Now that the war was over, I was eager to get into Germany and visit Fraulein's family. Fortunately my German was relatively fluent so I felt comfortable taking the course.

Living in Heidelberg was a traumatic experience. I had never experienced a place whose economy had totally collapsed: no services, nothing to buy, very little to eat. Our meals consisted primarily of vegetables, tomatoes, and potatoes, covered over with a thin meat sauce.

I was one of the twenty foreign students from all over Europe and America and 250 German students all of whom were eager for knowledge of the outside world and anxious to talk with their counterparts from other countries. Here I saw an interesting example of unorthodox teaching and how it affected the traditional German student.

We took two courses, both given in German, one in economics taught by a ponderous German scholar who lectured for two hours and then disappeared. The German students dutifully accepted this because he fitted into their stereotype of what a university professor should be. The other course was political science taught by a professor who started his first class by striding into the classroom, pointing to some poor student in the front row and asking where he had been in July 1944 when the German generals failed to execute a coup that was intended to kill Hitler and take over the government.

The German students, in general, were shocked at his question. This was not a proper university performance! Gradually they got used to him but never appeared comfortable and grumbled about his non-scholarly approach. They weren't accustomed to putting themselves into the academic dialogue. I never did find out whether they learned anything from him and his "unorthodox" ways.

When I was teaching my George School students, I felt like that German political science professor must have felt with his non-traditional teaching technique. I wondered whether my students actually learned more when they could identify with the subject matter and gained a better understanding of history's relevance to their daily lives.

I worked very hard with my George School students. Since I taught only one class I had a lot of spare time to devote to my slower students and their struggle broke my heart. Several would stay after class and I would work with them one-on-one. My goal was to give them confidence in their own abilities and help them overcome their particular academic problems.

Despite my efforts, I wasn't able to see any real improvement. I wanted to give them a higher grade for effort, to encourage them and reward their hard work. But the school was against that, pointing out that grading a student for effort was not fair to the student or their classmates. I could understand their reasoning but it always bothered me that a student should work so hard and not receive any recognition. My sense of a teacher's role was to awaken in the students a love of learning and help them develop a sense of their own worth even if they didn't measure up academically. If I had stayed longer in teaching, I am sure I would have found some ways to meet both of my goals without being unfair to other students.

I, like the rest of the faculty, attended the voluntary Quaker meetings as often as I could, but I was never able to accept that religion any more than any other. I was brought up an Episcopalian and at one point during the early 1950's, just before I started analysis and in my search for some answers, I tried very hard to become a Catholic. I took instruction for several months and regularly attended Mass, but couldn't develop the unquestioning faith in the existence of God that all religions require. The values underlying "Be true to yourself" and "Do unto others what you wilt be done to yourself" had always been important in my life, but I never could ascribe them to a belief in God.

I did like the simplicity of the Quaker meetings and the loving, principled life Quakers led. I think I had always sympathized with pacifist values. When I was very young, I was attracted to the pacifist philosophy of Pierre Van Paasen after I read his book, *Days of Our Years*. I found the Quakers were the only religious group I knew of that tried to live up to their Christian principles by refusing to serve in war combat operations. Instead they found alternate routes of service: being medics, volunteering for medical experimentation or for general service where the need was the greatest.

Toward the end of my first year at the George School I had not heard anything about whether or not they intended to keep me on, and I was getting increasingly upset over what I thought were my failings as a teacher. I found myself reading the same book my students were reading and always trying to stay one chapter ahead of them. This gave me a profound sense of inadequacy.

While I was debating whether teaching was right for me or not, I got a call from Gwen Carter, my history professor at Wellesley. Her friend, Louise Holborn, with whom she shared a house, had been alerted to a possible job in the Research and Analysis Branch of the Office of Strategic Services (OSS). She asked if I would be interested in applying. I said absolutely! Before I knew it, I had an interview lined up in Washington with Hajo Holborn, Louise's brother, who was head of OSS's Civil Affairs Division. He offered me a job at Grade P1 at the munificent annual salary of $1800! Since it was more than I was making, I knew I wouldn't starve.

Eventually the George School did offer me a full time teaching position in history but by that time I was committed to the OSS. I joined them in June 1944 after my teaching internship had come to an end, and immediately moved to Washington D.C. fully prepared for a new adventure.

The Office of Strategic Services had its origins in July 1941, five months before war was declared and the Japanese had attacked Pearl Harbor on December 7th. It was the brainchild of General William J. Donovan (then Colonel Donovan) who recognized the United States was desperately in need of a civilian intelligence agency. [1]

Donovan had persuaded President Franklin Roosevelt that there was a large vacuum in America's national security arsenal. At the time, the United States had several separate intelligence units, each serving a branch of the armed forces. In addition, the State and Treasury Departments, the FBI, and the Bureaus of Narcotics and Immigration each had their own foreign intelligence units. What was lacking, Donovan argued, was an overall civilian agency with both covert and overt responsibilities. President Roosevelt agreed and the OSS's predecessor, the Office of the Coordinator of Information, was set up in July 1941. The Office of Strategic Services was formally established the following June. At the conclusion of World War II, the Central Intelligence Agency was built on the OSS experience.

General Donovan reported directly to the president, but was in no way involved with the Cabinet. He had entrée into all the branches of the armed services as well as the State Department even though relationships were not always cordial between the various agencies. But most important, he had his own budget and complete freedom to hire and fire whomever he wanted within the civil service guidelines. General Donovan had both a successful Wall Street career and a unique wartime record in World War I as the leader of the Fighting 69th. A member of FDR's cabinet called Donovan "a man of unmitigated imagination and gall" who was "afraid of nobody and nothing, least of all a new concept." And an editor of the *Washington Post* described him as one who "is and was a genius. He has greater imagination than anyone I have ever known."

The OSS was divided into two major divisions: the super secret espionage branch, which played a significant role in the military phase of the war and the research and analysis division whose mandate was to produce estimates and reports on matters concerning the political and military direction of the war. I was assigned to work in the Research and Analysis branch along with some 400 other professionals, primarily academics. While I worked with the OSS I knew very little about any of the covert operations. It was only after I left and read some of the OSS history that I appreciated just how pivotal it had been to the total war effort.

The OSS record was outstanding. It performed a critical role in prosecuting the war in Europe against the Germans and Italians and eventually in Asia against the Japanese. Donovan was key to the entire operation. He negotiated the first agreement with the Russians allowing for the exchange of intelligence between the two countries. And he is credited with designing and successfully completing the major diversionary action in Eastern Europe to make the Germans believe that the Allied armies would attack Germany through the Balkans from bases in the Mediterranean. The mission is credited with shortening the war.

Also, Donovan's special operation forces, on instructions from General Dwight D. Eisenhower, captured Sardinia and Corsica, the all-important islands that helped the Allies acquire ports and airfields vital to their battles in Italy. And it was General Donovan who planned the operation in Eastern Europe that deprived the Germans of their essential source of Turkish chrome.

The Civil Affairs Office, where I worked, was charged with preparing handbooks to be used by our occupying forces in Germany. The handbooks were painstakingly prepared for each city including detailed maps of the city streets and location of critical services such as water and utilities. They contained lists of the inhabitants: those who had been active Nazis, those who were the natural leaders in the community, and those municipal officials who could be trusted.

The handbooks were written with the help of German refugees and specialists who had been recruited by OSS. What these refugees gave to this country was extraordinary: people such as the philosopher Herbert Marcuse, Franz Neumann, historian from Columbia University, Otto Kircheimer, an eminent international law scholar and Harold Lewis, from Howard University, historian and specialist in the German labor movement, and the only black member of the team. Similar handbooks were created for the far eastern theatre, especially Japan.

The segregated Washington of 1944 presented difficult problems to those of us with diverse staffs. Restaurants felt free to post signs in their windows, "We reserve the right to decide who shall eat at our premises." This made it difficult to have office parties outside our building. We were lucky to find one Chinese restaurant in the city that allowed us to have a private room on the second floor when we wanted to get together.

Washington remained segregated after the war. In the summer of 1948, when I returned to Washington and wanted to lunch with Harold, one of my African-American OSS colleagues, the only place where we could eat together was at a YWCA in northeast Washington. I took a taxi there to meet him and the cabbie turned to me and asked whether I knew where I was going. I said, of course. He gave me a look of disgust that said, only a white trash woman would eat in a black restaurant in northeast Washington!

When I arrived at OSS in 1944 the handbook project was winding down. On the day of my arrival Hajo Holborn went on a much-deserved six weeks vacation and his assistant, Phoebe Morrison, was left in charge. I went to work for her. Phoebe was a Yale Law School graduate and an international lawyer who worked at the law school as an assistant to Dr. Edwin Borchard.

A renowned and respected international lawyer, Borchard was editor of the papers of John Basset Moore who, at the turn of the century, had achieved eminence as the American member of the International Court of Justice. Borchard had been a member of the controversial America First group that tried to keep America out of the war. Some of the members were reported to have admired the efficiency of the Nazis and, in some cases, to hold anti-Semitic views. Phoebe didn't share these sentiments but admired Borchard as an international law scholar.

I quickly found a place to live in Washington and moved in with a Wellesley classmate and two other women. We shared a house on Hawthorne Place, just off McArthur Boulevard, at a monthly rent for each of us of $35.00, easily affordable with my P-1 salary of $1800.

Commuting to work was easy. Washington had trolleys at the time and one went along McArthur Boulevard right to my office at the foot of Twenty-third Street. I had also brought with me my father's 1934 Chevrolet with a rumble seat and a right hand drive that he had installed because of his deafness. His left ear was his better ear so he could hear people talk more easily with the steering wheel on the right. It was a great car that used very little gas. I shared it with my sister, Betty, who was also in Washington at the time. We didn't use it very often but it was a big help and enabled us to get around Washington in spite of gas rationing.

Phoebe had turned our office into an international law office that provided advice on international law and intelligence analysis to the State Department, the Army and any of the other branches of government that needed our expertise. She was a wonderful woman, single and the only girl in a family of three. She lived in Silver Springs with her unmarried brother, Ben, who worked at the Department of Agriculture. Phoebe was the first person I had ever met who talked frankly about her difficulty in getting along with her family. I wasn't conscious of how relaxing and refreshing it was to be with someone else who didn't camouflage her negative feelings about her parents. Somewhere inside of me I always knew I had to get away from the stuffy authoritarian atmosphere of my family, but it wasn't something I talked about until I met Phoebe. With Phoebe, I felt free to open up for the first time.

My work, for the most part, was not involved with any super secret missions as far as I ever knew. Because I was able to read German and French, I was also responsible for analyzing intelligence that we could glean from the foreign press in neutral countries like Switzerland, Lichtenstein, Andorra. We were particularly interested in intelligence that involved troop movements, the treatment of captured partisan forces, or other relevant data that related to the security of our Allied forces. We were also particularly concerned about the status of our own OSS agents, should they be captured, as well as the Partisan resistance forces that had sprung up in much of occupied Europe. We wanted to see what the international law precedents were that defined these various categories of wartime personnel and also how these forces were being treated in this war.

My job also included writing weekly situation reports on the data we were gathering that we sent to the State Department officers working in the same arena. I thought it might be useful if I met with my State Department counterparts to find out what they were interested in.

I went to the department, introduced myself, and asked how they wanted to use our reports. I am sure I came across exactly as I was—a naïve freshly minted college graduate full of enthusiasm. I am afraid I didn't generate any particular respect from the department's "old hands" and I quickly learned the State Department had little use for the OSS. I am sure they were certainly more suspicious of the information we sent them after that they discovered it had been written by a brash young kid not yet dry behind the ears. I thought all of it was pretty funny and proceeded to go happily about my business hoping someone would find my reports useful. Ah, the obliviousness of youth!

I found it amazing how easy it was to put together isolated bits of intelligence and then connect the dots. Once you had an overall view of what you were looking for, the key was to uncover enough dots. I understood the strict security that was so necessary at the OSS. They insisted we, as employees, refrain from talking in public about our jobs no matter how innocuous the conversation, or however veiled and generalized our comments might be.

The OSS also had strict regulations on who could see their material even when it was developed from public sources. But in wartime it was often urgent to find ways to get around the regulations. I remember one Foreign Economic Board member who needed some information we had but officially we couldn't let him see it. We knew his request was important and we needed to find a way to respond. Our solution was to leave the material on our desk when we went out to lunch and then invite him to come to our office during the lunch hour. Phoebe and I always found a way to skin a cat if that was our only hope of getting the work done.

The last major task we undertook was to brief the Nurenberg prosecuting attorneys on the international law precedents for the war crimes trials. Some of the questions we tried to answer were how were crimes against humanity defined, had they ever been prosecuted before, were there any precedents for the international tribunal that was being created to try the Nazi officials who had participated in these crimes. Our work was based entirely on public information source materials, but in order to get our report to the army war crimes prosecutor in Germany in ample time, we had to classify the document Top Secret so that it could go by courier. I often wonder whether the rationale for classifying many government documents today is based on just as flimsy and expedient grounds that have so little to do with security and much to do with protecting bureaucracy, or in our case, getting around bureaucracy.

D-Day had brought about the unconditional surrender of Germany and the war in the Pacific was clearly moving towards a similar conclusion. The dropping of the atom bombs on Hiroshima and Nagasaki, with all their horrific consequences, brought the Japanese to a similar unconditional surrender. The OSS was disbanded and replaced in 1947 by the Central Intelligence Agency (CIA), established by the National Security Act.

The research analysts in the Research and Analysis Branch of the OSS were returning to their universities or accepting new job offers. In the summer of 1945, Phoebe took over as the executive director of a new foundation just being started and largely funded by the Regnery family, of Chicago, who are still active in the conservative right today. The only thing we knew about the Regnerys then, however, was that they owned a profitable window shade factory.

The creation of the foundation was one of the very early steps taken by the right wing of the Republican Party to establish an intellectual basis for their conservative philosophies. They wanted to counter the writings and pronouncements of liberal think tanks such as the Brookings Institution, the Rand Corporation and countless others that had been set up by scholars who believed deeply in the power of research and analysis as a tool to bring about social and economic justice. Their work was very high caliber and objective. Their liberal bias showed up mainly in the research questions they posed to themselves and wanted to explore.

The foundation that hired Phoebe assumed she held the same right wing sentiments as they did because of her association with Edwin Borchard. But, first and foremost, Phoebe was a scholar and resigned when she realized they were really interested in creating a foundation dominated by right wing concerns.

As the time approached for me to leave the OSS, I talked a lot with Phoebe about what I wanted to do after the war. My original thought was to go on with teaching and get a Ph.D. in history or international affairs. But, as I talked it over with her, I found the law also fascinated me. While still at the OSS, I had taken a few law courses at night to see if I liked it. I found myself increasingly excited about law and realized I could pursue my growing international interests just as easily through that route, so I decided on law school.

Phoebe Morrison and my experience at the OSS had a major influence on my decision; but as I look back, there were probably other subtle influences at work. For several generations, there had been prominent lawyers on both sides of my family. Uncle Livy was a lawyer although he never practiced, and, of course, there was Aunt Rosalie! I am sure subliminally she was a big factor in my decision. Finally, today I recognize that law is an accepted way to be confrontational since law itself is adversarial; and I think, for me, it was a positive way of managing the anger and hostility that had been building up in me over the years. Though subconscious, I am sure this was another major force in selecting law as my future career.

Notes

1. Much of the material about the OSS referred to in this chapter is drawn from Anthony Cave Brown's *Wild Bill Donovan, the Last Hero* (Time Books, 1982) and supplemented by my own experience at the OSS.

Changing Directions

When I made my decision to go to law school, I was told it was a difficult career choice for women and that after I graduated I would find it hard to get a job practicing law. That didn't stop me. I thought, somehow, I would be different and wouldn't experience what others had, so I applied to Yale. Phoebe Morrison wrote the dean, Wesley Sturgis, and I went up to New Haven for my interview.

I was oblivious to any possible problems about getting into law school and I didn't have any special anxieties about the interview. I don't remember whom I talked to but I do remember coming away thinking Yale would be a good place to be. I'm sure the fact that Phoebe had paved the way made a difference because shortly after I returned to Washington I received my acceptance notice.

My housemates were also moving on to other jobs, so leaving the Washington house didn't present any problems. I packed up my belongings—pretty much the same things I had when I went to college: clothes, books, records and a record player– and took off for New Haven about a month after school had started. I wasn't able to wind up my job at the OSS any sooner. Fortunately, I missed only the orientation for incoming first year students so I didn't feel I had lost anything because of my late start.

I hadn't talked with mother about going to law school because I knew she was only interested in me getting married, and not in my pursuing a professional career. I did toy briefly with the idea of asking her for help with my tuition, but this was just wishful thinking on my part. I knew she believed she had fulfilled her educational responsibilities to me by paying for Wellesley. She had always told me in her blunt and direct manner that any financial obligations to me ended there.

So, in the end, I didn't ask her for help with my tuition and she certainly didn't offer. Fortunately, I was able to work out the finances for my freshman year. We had worked six days a week at the OSS and never took vacations, so I had a considerable amount of leave time saved up. At the time, government employees were able to cash in their accrued annual vacation time, so this, plus my unused sick leave, meant my OSS paychecks kept coming and paid for much of my first year. Plus, I was very frugal. I found I could eat lunch at the Yale Commons for thirty-five cents and dinner for sixty-five cents.

During my second year I had scholarships or loans and this helped me pay for the rest of my law school tuition. All I really needed to augment my finances was twenty-five dollars a month, so I went to Uncle Livy and he readily agreed to give me this. Livy was always generous with his money if he believed it was for a serious purpose and I knew what I wanted to do. He also was the one who made it financially possible for me to take a semester off to attend summer school in Zurich.[1] He agreed with me that such a trip right after the war would be both educational and interesting. This was the time our government wanted to encourage students, artists, and community organizations such as the American Farm Women of the World (AFWW) to go abroad.

We sailed over on the *Marine Tiger*, a liberty ship the government had slightly refurbished for this purpose, and they invited anthropologist Margaret Mead to be on board and conduct orientation sessions for us. I remember her reminding us not to make quantitative comparisons—our apples are redder, our trees are taller—but to look at life in Europe as equal, but different. The trip was a good break from the high tension of law school and right after my return I resumed my studies.

Women law students were housed with the other women graduate students at Hill House, a large building close to the law school. Lucy Kraus, who was very young and had just graduated from a small southern university, was assigned to me as my roommate. When we met she asked where I had gone to college and when I told her I was Wellesley '43, she visibly blanched. I later found out she thought I said I was forty-three and to her that meant I was over the hill.

There were only six women out of the 300 students enrolled in the law school—exactly two in each class! And there were no women on the teaching faculty. Phoebe had been a Research Assistant to Professor Borchard and was not considered part of the faculty. Still, I didn't feel any overt prejudice and I accepted the law school's admission policy that preference should be given to young men who were just returning from the service.

The Yale Law School had been admitting women since the early 1930s but I don't know if they had a quota then or not. However, I was shocked to learn that in 1969, Hillary Rodham Clinton was one of twenty-seven women out of a class of 235 and she called that a breakthrough. [2] I found this disappointing because I always assumed the quotas I experienced had been lifted after the war. Yet here they were, still going strong, in the late 1960s.

When I was in law school, even though there were limits on women applicants, we weren't considered a curiosity nor were we the subject of crude jokes, as I'm told women were at other law schools, especially Harvard. Harvard didn't even permit women to apply for admission until 1956 and from what I've heard, their early years were not easy. Mrs. Clinton quotes one Harvard law professor, on hearing that Hillary was trying to decide between Harvard and its closest competitor, Yale, as saying "Well first of all, we don't have any close competitors and second, we don't need any more women at Harvard." [3] And this was said in 1969, fifteen years after Harvard first admitted women to its law school! Yet the world is seldom consistent. It was also the 1960s when the male law students at Yale broke the barrier of various law firms' resistance to hiring women by refusing to be recruited by them if they didn't accept women.[4]

I found the faculty and students at Yale respectful and friendly except for the Dean, Wesley Sturgis. He taught an introductory course in legal writing as well as corporate law and I had the feeling he shared the anti-woman attitudes of the traditional male corporate world. But I never remember Dean Sturgis, or any other faculty member, directing hostile questions to us or in any way trying to embarrass us, as I heard had happened in other law schools when they began to admit women. Gene Rostow and Walton Hamilton were particularly gracious and helpful to us as we began what turned out for me to be a disastrous job-hunting process. And the other students, for the most part, were gracious and helpful as well.

I had little sense of being discriminated against because I was a woman. No student ever cut me off in mid-sentence, disrespected what I had to say, or ignored my presence; all issues I experienced later in my career when I was the only woman in an all male environment.

Of course, there were boundaries. We weren't allowed in at Mory's, the famous eating and carousing place for Yalies, but that wasn't a big issue. I remember only one fellow student asking me a hostile question. He wanted to know why women were there "taking the place of a serviceman who needed to get on with his life." The fact that we also wanted a career and, in my case, had spent time in government wartime service was lost on him. I also remember another incident when an exceedingly attractive woman complained to me that the male students didn't take her seriously. I told her I had the opposite problem. They took me too seriously and didn't see me as a woman. Perhaps it was because I didn't see myself that way or perhaps it was because I didn't know how to be a woman *and* a law student at the same time.

Law school was the most exhilarating, stimulating and intellectual experience I have ever had. In the 1920s, Yale was in the forefront of what was called "Legal Realism." Realists believed that law without a relationship to social realities produced a backward status quo of little value to a fast moving and changing society so characteristic of the United States.[5]

The law school and the legal realists had a common mission: to produce more competent and socially responsible practitioners, more informed and effective judges and administrators, and more carefully framed and effective proposals for reform. Public activism by the faculty in both legal and political issues was considered very important, and the school placed a major emphasis on public law. The curriculum was interdisciplinary and included courses that had a direct relationship to the humanities and social sciences.[6]

Robert M. Hutchins, who served briefly as Dean in 1927, contributed to Yale's increasing sociological approach to the law. He linked the law school to the university's new social science research center, and recruited psychologists, economists and other non-lawyers to the faculty.[7] A few years ago the law school dean, Harold Hongju Koh, wrote a letter to the Yale alumnae and said: "I can think of nothing more critical than protecting and expanding the law's role as a constructive tool for unleashing human potential and promoting our shared humanity. These have been and will always be our unwavering values since the school began in 1824." It used to be said that Harvard sought to train lawyers, while Yale's goal was to train judges and policy makers. I think that is an accurate observation, one with which I wholeheartedly agree.

The law school also had a deep commitment to using the intellect to make the world a better place. What drove their teaching was an emphasis on excellence and stressing action and humanity. And they taught me to love the elegance of the law and how it could be used to achieve practical reform. This was the environment I walked into. And I was the perfect student for their mission: young, idealistic and wanting to save the world. Yet, on the other hand, no one wanted to hang on more tightly to certainty than I did. I really believed there was something called "the law." I believed you just had to find it and then apply it to the situation you were dealing with. Yale's goal was to disabuse young people like myself of such a mechanistic concept of the law and I was young, malleable and loved the challenge they forced me to confront.

Thanks to Yale, I learned that law *was* a living, breathing and consistently changing system dependent on human beings to interpret and apply it. I came out of law school a convert, speaking pure law school legalese. I was an idealist and for good or ill have continued to be that ever since.

I made mostly A's, wound up a member of COIF, the law school equivalent of Phi Beta Kappa, and graduated tenth in my class. I didn't do that well at Wellesley and hadn't even made Wellesley Scholar, one of the lowest academic honors they offered. Clearly I had matured and grown up since my college days. Because of my first year grades, I was invited to join the *Law Journal* and the next year was very proud to be elected managing editor, a testament by my peers that I was acceptable to work with. I wrote several *Law Journal Comments* and two of my full-length articles involving international and administrative law were published in the *Journal*. Clearly I had found my niche!

Of course, I took most of the so-called bread and butter courses that every law student needs to pass the bar: contracts, torts, real property, federal procedure, criminal law, corporate law, and tax law. But I was

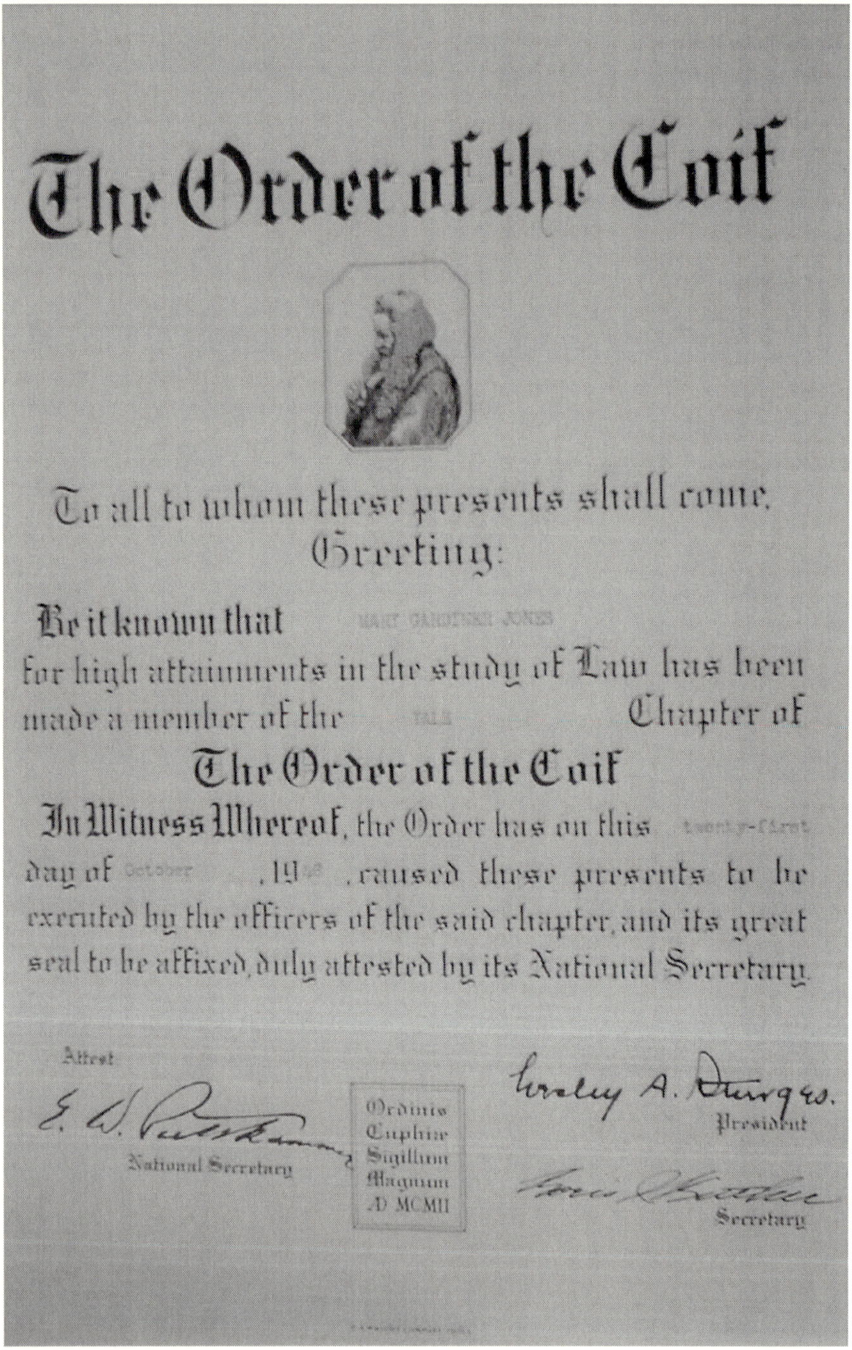

The Order of the Coif

To all to whom these presents shall come,
Greeting:

Be it known that MARY GARDINER JONES
for high attainments in the study of Law has been
made a member of the YALE Chapter of

The Order of the Coif

In Witness Whereof, the Order has on this twenty-first
day of October, 19[illegible], caused these presents to be
executed by the officers of the said chapter, and its great
seal to be affixed, duly attested by its National Secretary.

Attest

National Secretary

Ordinis
Cuphiae
Sigillum
Magnum
AD MCMII

Wesley A. Sturges
President

Secretary

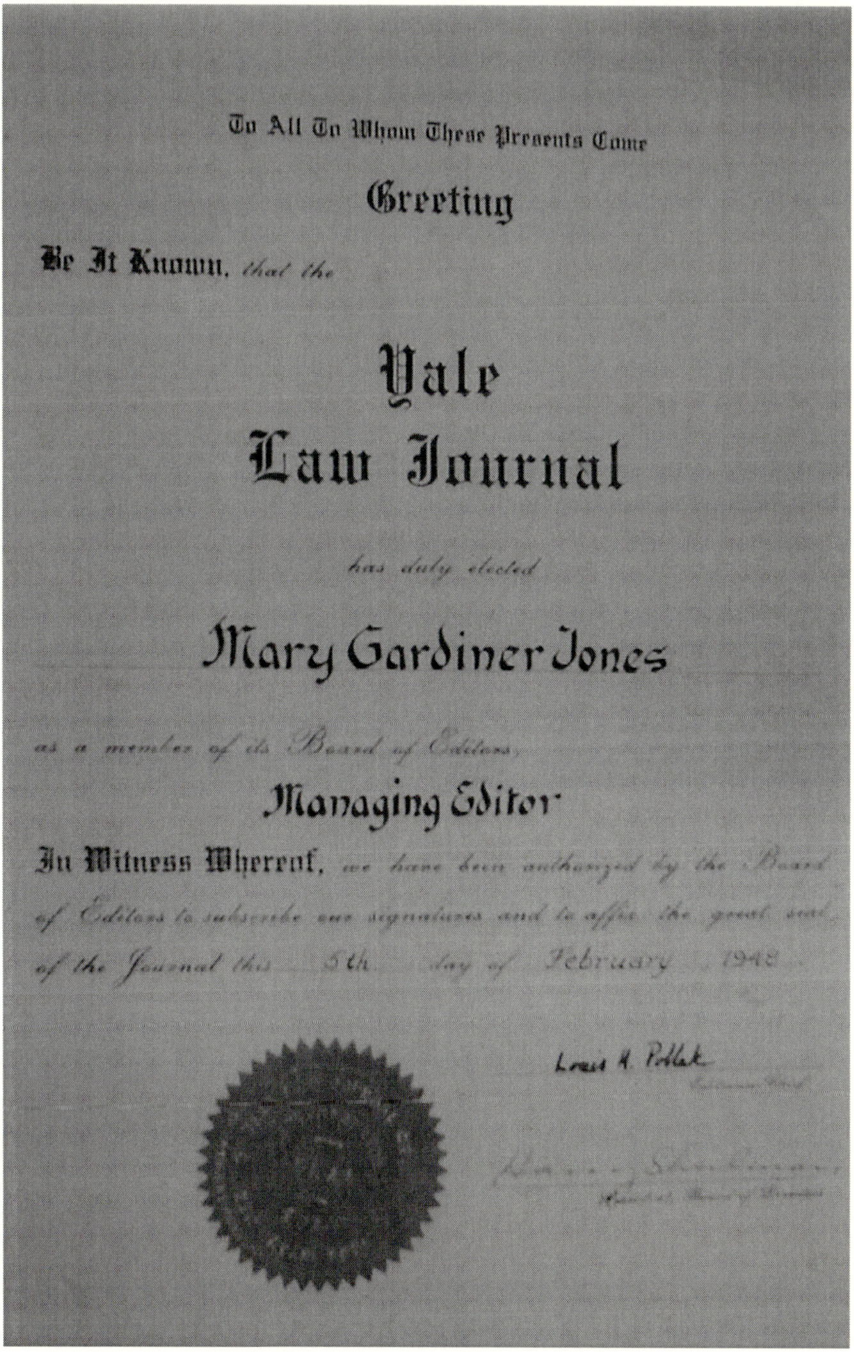

To All To Whom These Presents Come

Greeting

Be It Known, that the

Yale
Law Journal

has duly elected

Mary Gardiner Jones

as a member of its Board of Editors,

Managing Editor

In Witness Whereof, we have been authorized by the Board of Editors to subscribe our signatures and to affix the great seal of the Journal this 5th day of February 1948.

Louis H. Pollak

always fascinated by policy and very early I found myself gravitating toward the many publicly-oriented courses: international law, international human and economic rights, constitutional law, antitrust and one I remember, the Legal Problems of River Valleys.

Following my international law experience working with Phoebe at the OSS, and at her suggestion and with her help, I took an honors course with Professor Borchard who by now was an emeritus professor at the law school. He suggested that for my honors work I work with him to edit the papers of John Basset Moore, a preeminent international lawyer at the State Department and a member of the Permanent Court of International Justice at the turn of the century. I jumped at the chance. I was eager to do original research in a field and period so critical to world peace and it fed into my history background and my growing interest in international law.

Moore's papers were voluminous and fascinating. He was a tireless recorder of everything he read and did: the streets he walked to get to his office, whom he talked to en route and about what subject, what he had eaten that day and what each item had cost. Among his trivia were his comments about the international scene that surrounded him, the international policy positions of the State Department and comments on the books he had read. He had a unique way of analyzing international law, basing it significantly on actual international practices.

His papers, therefore, were an invaluable source about the international work of the State Department, but, unfortunately, I never did make much of a dent in them in the one semester I devoted to them. I presume they are still in the dusty law school archives in the same boxes they had been shipped in, waiting for some eager law scholar to finish examining them.

Like serious students everywhere, my classmates and I spent a great deal of time discussing the many international issues confronting the country: the new United Nations, the budding Human Rights Declaration, and Point IV of the General Agreement on World Trade and Tariffs that dealt with international development.

Our discussions about the Declaration of Human Rights centered on the United Nations General Assembly debates on the relative importance of political vs. social and economic rights that we followed avidly. Under the masterful guidance of Eleanor Roosevelt, the UN General

Assembly did pass the Declaration of Human Rights on December 10, 1948, but it was based solely on political rights with a promise of developing a second declaration to focus on social and economic rights. It wasn't until 1966 that the Declaration of Social, Economic and Cultural Rights was finally enacted by the General Assembly.

As we were debating all this, several of us got together and decided to put on a conference about human rights. We invited the Ambassador of India to be our keynote speaker. I was delegated to call for the ambassador at his hotel and escort him to the law school. Dutifully I presented myself at the desk and was told to go upstairs to his suite. When I arrived he was very polite and after a little conversation he asked me if I would like to see the rest of his apartment. In all innocence, I said yes. The next thing I knew he was chasing me around the bedroom while I was thinking I can't alienate him or he won't come to the conference. I managed to extricate myself from that uncomfortable situation—I was faster than he was—and duly delivered him to the law school. I learned much later that he was recalled to India. My guess is he had made this his ordinary operating procedure!

In my last year of law school the real world reared its ugly head, and it was time for me to leave the ivory tower and nail down a job. The custom was to begin looking for a job in the fall of the year in which you were to graduate. Since we had completed six semesters in two years, we were not able to use the summers between semesters to get much needed experience and explore various job opportunities.

I wanted to practice in New York City, for me, the epicenter of my profession and where I wanted to be. I planned my search systematically and armed myself with lists of the New York law firms in each of the various Wall Street buildings. For the first time in my life I came up against flagrant discrimination. Most law firms simply did not hire women and told me so to my face. In 1948, this was not against the law.

My routine consisted of presenting myself to the receptionist, whose job it was to assign the applicant to whomever was interviewing law students that day. But I seldom got past her. Most were unfailingly polite but would say quite casually, "Oh, Miss Jones, the firm doesn't hire women lawyers."

A few firms weren't so upfront. They had a policy of interviewing all comers. I assume this meant Black and Hispanic students as well but I don't know this. So I went into each interview armed with good grades and high expectations. In most cases, the interviewing partner said nothing about the firm's policy on women. In some instances, the partner or associate was more forthcoming. They always took great pains to point out that refusing to hire women was not a violation of the New York State anti discrimination laws.

One partner at Cadwallader and Taft obviously distressed, said, "Oh, Miss Jones, if I suggested you as a candidate my partners would have a heart attack." Looking around at all those white bewhiskered firm partners in their formal morning suits, whose portraits made up a kind of wallpaper hanging side by side in the reception room, I had to agree. I couldn't imagine any of them welcoming a woman lawyer into their inner sanctum.

I went to Lord Day and Lord, a much respected admiralty firm, thinking surely they would be interested in a young law graduate with expertise in trade and international law. Not at all. I was met with the explanation that "our young lawyers have to go into the holds of ships to interview ship personnel", at which point they trailed off believing it was self-evident that a young woman could not be asked to do that! I still wonder which of their lawyers, young or old, would ever go into the hold of a ship to gather evidence. However, I figured it was not my role to get into a fight over this since clearly this had nothing to do with why they didn't want a woman lawyer in their midst.

A final memorable experience—among the many humiliating, hilarious or heart-breaking experiences (depending on my mood at the time) was an encounter with a firm specializing in maritime, aviation and railroad transportation law. The firm listed one woman associate among their lawyers. For the umpteenth time I presented myself to one of their partners and for the umpteenth time I gave my spiel. It was good enough to hold his attention but when I finished he looked at me and said, "Oh, Miss Jones, I really would like to hire you but you see our lawyers have to travel with the client and you understand, Miss Jones, women in railroad sleeping cars, it just wouldn't do." I didn't say anything. He hesitated for a moment, looked quizzical and said: "We have one woman lawyer in our aviation department." That seemed to stymie him for a moment and then he brightened, the legal mind at work, "But you see, Miss Jones, that's airplanes." End interview. What could I say?

So, Thanksgiving came and went, and most of the other "A" students had been hired. By Christmas the "B" students had nailed down their jobs, leaving the "C" students to spend the winter trying to see what few crumbs were left.

I continued slogging the streets, going to see law firms that were not on the law school list but had offices in the various buildings I had already visited. It got to be May and still no bites. I had seen over fifty firms and not a hint of a job. I kept wondering what my problem was. Did I come across as too earnest or somber? Was there something about my personality that grated against the male psyche? Perhaps I had an "attitude" that came across as antagonistic to men. After all, I told myself, I hadn't had many serious relationships while I was in college or in Washington or in law school, for that matter.

As a matter of fact, in law school I seemed to relate best to the homosexual students, which wasn't particularly surprising since my Uncle Livy, the most important man in my life, was homosexual and I had learned to please him. My father was too remote and his deafness complicated his isolation, so obviously I had no real experience of being loved or cherished by a heterosexual male.

My major goal became to avoid getting a chip on my shoulder. I continued to cling to the notion that there are always two sides to an issue and somehow somewhere there was a job waiting for me.

In mid-May I heard that the law firm of Donovan Leisure Newton Lombard and Irvine was coming to Yale to recruit. Apparently they had hired someone from my class who at the last minute had changed his mind and went to another firm. I signed up to see the partner. Naturally, I didn't tell him that I had already seen one of their other partners who had turned me down on the grounds that the firm was a litigating firm and women in litigation, etc, etc. We talked. After a while Roy McDonald, the interviewing partner, said he thought his senior partner, William J. Donovan, might be interested in talking with me. The next day found me on the doorstep of Number 2 Wall Street where the firm was located asking to see General Donavan. After a very few minutes they said the general was in and would be happy to see me.

I don't know what I expected. I had never met the general while I was at the OSS but I certainly didn't expect to see this slightly paunchy, mild-mannered man of medium height with a soft voice and the most penetrating blue eyes I had ever seen. Certainly neither by his appearance nor manner did he seem to be the man who earned the nickname of "Wild Bill" which was reportedly given to him by his troops in World War I while he was leading the Fighting 69th. It is recorded that he wanted his troops to do more in a particular situation and when his troops balked, someone said, "Hell Bill, we ain't as wild as you."

We immediately engaged in a broad conversation. We talked about Radio Free Europe, the timidity of Secretary of State John Foster Dulles' policies and other subjects that I have since forgotten. I was a committed internationalist so we shared a lot of common concerns about our foreign policy. And he was also open and personal. He told me about his daughter, about my age, who had been killed in an automobile accident. It was only much later that I read he was absolutely devoted to her and was emotionally crushed when she was killed. Now I come along: his daughter's age, active, bright and probably looking for a solid father figure. We took to each other immediately. I always marvel at how powerful our underlying emotions can be and how so often they play a significant role in many of the decisions we make.

General Donovan said the magic words: I was hired! For part of my time I was to be his assistant, and for the other part I was to be a regular member of the legal staff. Finally, my job crusade bore fruit; I was to be a real practicing member of the profession I had chosen as my life career.

Notes

1. We attended classes for three semesters a year so as to finish in two years.
2. Hillary Rodham Clinton, *Living History*, (Simon and Shuster, 2003), p. 44
3. *Ibid.* p. 38.
4. Shades of Aunt Rosalie's "Bless the men, we couldn't have done it without them?"
5. Robert M. Gordon, "Professors and Policymakers: Yale Law School Faculty in the New Deal and After" in Anthony Kronman, Editor, *History of the Yale Law School,* (Yale University Press, 2004), pp. 90-1.
6. Anthony Kronman, *op.cit.* "Introduction" p. xi.
7. Robert M. Gordon, *op.cit.* p. 84.

Entering a Man's World

In the fall of 1948, when I started to work at Donovan Leisure, it was a mid-sized law firm with about fifty lawyers. I was a little anxious, but excited and happy to be starting on my law career. Of course, I arrived on the first day at the firm way too early.I didn't understand about partner's hours at that time, so the partner I was supposed to report to had yet to arrive. One of my fellow lawyers—a big blond six footer—later told me that on his first day he had hidden in the men's room for at least half an hour before daring to show his face. On my first day, I found myself working in the library when the partner who originally turned me down came in and welcomed me. I had been curious about whether or not he would remember me and he did. He was very gracious and neither of us referred to our first meeting.

I shared a small office with a fellow lawyer, John Seiberling, a conscientious tax lawyer who, a few months later, when his wife was having their first child, was hard at work at the office claiming he was more useful at the office than he would be at the hospital! I hadn't been in the office more than a couple of weeks when my fellow lawyers came to me wanting to straighten out how I felt about going through doors ahead of them. They said they didn't care, but didn't want to be running into me if they went ahead to open the door. I thought that was very sensitive, and I appreciated their candor. I think we decided that whoever happened to get there first would just proceed.

So, that was my first introduction to being in a total man's world. It is interesting, after all the difficulties I had trying to enter these sacrosanct law firms, that once I was let in I never again felt any discrimination.

Everyone I had contact with was very nice, but I was insecure and didn't quite know how to behave.

The only other gender issue I ran into was one night while working late. One of the partners, who lived very close to my apartment, wanted to escort me home. I vigorously objected. I told him I didn't want to cause any waves because I was woman. He said to me, "Now, Mary, you are both a woman and a lawyer and you should expect to be treated as both." I was touched. He was right and I let him escort me home. But I struggled with that "duality" in my own mind for a long time.

I was happy about being back in New York City and starting my new career, but first I had to find an apartment. Fortunately, Margie Slocum, the other woman in my class at law school, was also coming to New York, and we decided to look for a place together. Margie had finally found a job with a two-man law firm, which didn't last long because she didn't like their small town practice. She found a non-legal job and didn't get back into the legal world until some 20 years later when she became Dean of Admissions at New York Law School. Mary Date, my Japanese-American friend from the George School, was already in New York still working at Altman's, and was interested in joining us. Given the price of apartments, we welcomed having another roommate.

Then came a rude awakening. My Uncle Livy invited me to meet him for cocktails at the Pierre Hotel and fixing me with his eyes said, "Now, Mary, you have to take care of your mother." It was only later that I realized he was scared to death that mother would want to live with him now that "Honey" had died and she was alone. He wanted to make certain that didn't happen. Ann was married, Betty was abroad, and I was the single daughter, so clearly he thought that was my role and I accepted it without question.

I also suspect my mother was doing her usual pleading of poverty because of the rent she was paying for her apartment on 66th Street. Her claim of poverty always irritated me. She had little sense of what it was like to work. I remember once Betty and I were kidding her when she was talking about Livy being so poor when he had a yacht and homes in New York, Long Island and Palm Beach! She got very angry and burst out: "I don't understand you children! You are both earning salaries (I was working that summer at a New York bank) and your poor Uncle Livy is living off his capital!"

Always the dutiful daughter, despite my periodic rebellious outbursts, I listened to Livy and invited mother to join us. I began looking for an apartment that would be large enough for four of us and found one at 16 East 96th Street. Curiously enough it was the same building I had lived in as a child.

The big apartments we lived in then had been divided into two, but even as smaller apartments they were ample for our needs. We had a large high ceiling living room, tiny foyer, two bedrooms, kitchen and a den. I turned the den into my room, as it was big enough to accommodate my hide-a-bed, piano and books. I gave the double bedroom to my roommates and the single bedroom to mother.

We shared our $200 monthly rental which has to be seen in the context of our salaries in those days. I was making $3600 a year and I am sure that Mary and Margie's salaries were even lower. My mother paid her full share even though she wasn't there all year around. She continued with her life, going to Palm Beach with Livy in the winter and to her house in Cold Spring Harbor for the summer, so she was only with us three months in the fall and another three in the spring.

I found it strangely familiar to be back in the old New York neighborhood where I had grown up and seeing that it was very much the same. Mr. Celentano, the green grocer, was there; Mr. Lipshutz was still operating the newspaper stand; and even Mr. Schlossberg, the tailor, was still in business. Of course they didn't recognize me and I am sure they wondered who this strange woman was who greeted them like old friends. Now with all my ducks in a row, I happily started work.

General Donovan—everyone called him that—had founded the firm in 1929 and wanted it to operate like a country law firm. The General's ideas were unique: his lawyers were to be well rounded and active in their communities; he did not expect them to work long hours every night, and he insisted they all take a full month's vacation. It was also stipulated they must take their vacation all at once so they could take advantage of a thirty-day chunk of time. This was anathema to one partner, Vern Carnihan, who had six children at home and kept insisting that staying at home for him was no vacation!

In the 1940s, the Donovan firm with fifty lawyers was considered mid-sized. Some law firms had 100 lawyers but few, if any, had branch offices in other cities or abroad. None of the law firms I knew, even the larger ones, were anything like the commercial institutions they are today.

The legal profession has drastically changed. Today a firm of 100 lawyers is considered small to mid-sized and almost all of the big firms have branches in other cities and abroad. So far as I can tell, billable hours have virtually replaced the law firms' emphasis on quality that was so prominent in my day. However, the attitude towards law as a business and a good way to make money was already in the air.

When I first entered the profession, I was naïve, idealistic and awestruck at being admitted to the Bar. I took the lawyer's status as an officer of the court literally and believed that the effective functioning of the law depended on how attorneys conducted themselves. I was quickly disabused of this notion when I was sworn in by a New York City Municipal Judge, whose closing remarks to us were on the need to find clients to support the lifestyle we hoped to have!

Equally sobering for me was taking the professional oath required for admission to the New York Bar. It was 1948, the eve of the Cold War, and America's concerns were focused on the threat of Communism at home and abroad. The oath we were asked to take committed us to support the Constitution but also *not to overthrow the government.* What had been omitted, however, was the phrase that usually followed, "by violence." I believed I was being asked to swear I would not seek to change any clause in the Constitution regardless of whether or not the means I used were peaceful. I was in a dilemma. I went directly to the General and said I didn't see how, in good conscience, I could take this oath because I believed it was unconstitutional. The General agreed that the oath was probably unconstitutional but said that at this point in my career I shouldn't ruin my professional life by challenging it. I took the oath but felt badly that at the first challenge to my ideals I had caved in so easily.

I found my fellow attorneys friendly and comfortable to work with. There were nine of us freshly minted lawyers and we shared the tribulations of inexperienced lawyers who were now working in the real world. My first assignment was an issue in bankruptcy law. I had been in the firm library on a Friday afternoon (which I immediately recognized was a bad idea) when one of the partners came in, grabbed me by the shoulders and said he had a rush job that needed to be done immediately. I spent the entire weekend trying to locate New York's bankruptcy law and the section involving the question he had posed. Since bankruptcy law was one of the practical elective courses I skipped while I was in law school, I should have known it would come back to haunt me! Monday morning, sheep-faced, I had to tell the partner I didn't have an answer to his question. That partner never called me again.

In those early days I also found myself working for another partner, and turned in a memorandum labeled "draft." He called me into his office and told me in no uncertain terms he was not interested in receiving a draft and he wanted only a finished product. He returned my draft and I made sure that never happened again. (Incidentally, later in my career, I never permitted my staff to get away with that subterfuge either).

On another occasion, I worked for several months on a twenty one-page memorandum trying to disentangle the corporate relationships of the multi-national German corporation, I.G. Farben and a large Swiss bank, I.G. Chemie. When I finished and turned my memorandum in to the litigating partner, he read it and said, "I think you will find that if you reorganize this material chronologically it will make more sense." I was crestfallen, but when I did what he suggested I realized he was absolutely right. All of a sudden the facts I had developed began to clear up many of the corporate interrelationships we were trying to untangle. So, in time, and after many mistakes, I learned my way around the business of being a lawyer in a prestigious New York firm.

A large percentage of my work was for General Donovan. The General when I knew him was stocky with thinning white hair, a gentle voice and the most penetrating blue eyes I had ever seen. He lived in an apartment on Sutton Place in New York City with a butler in attendance. His wife, Ruth, spent a good deal of her time with their son, David, at their farm in Berryville.

The General was the real force in the firm and certainly the boss when he chose to interest himself in the mundane practice of law. Mostly, however, the General occupied himself with national security issues and foreign policy. He had little respect for former Secretary of State Dean Acheson and thought Acheson should have toughened his stand towards the USSR and their allies. In one speech he wrote that the United States ought to react strongly to any incident we had with the Russians by taking some Russian diplomats as hostages.

Julio Nunez, who did some occasional work for the General, joined me in urging him not to publicize this position. The United States Declaration of Human Rights and the Nuremberg trials of Nazi war criminals had made clear that taking hostages was not consistent with either international law or the Human Rights Declaration. The General wasn't pleased with our suggestion. After he gave the speech he called us in and said, "I thought you both would like to know, I made the point but I didn't use the word hostage."

I learned about leadership first hand while working with General Donovan. He was a quiet man and his outward manner was in sharp contrast to the nickname of 'Wild Bill' that his Fighting 69th troops had given him during World War I. But as I got to know him I learned to appreciate that name. He had such great self-confidence and inner authority that had he ever said to me, "Mary, I think the solution is for you to jump out that window," I probably would have done it. He exuded an aura of knowing what should be done and was the kind of person you trusted implicitly and knew he would probably be right behind you.

I co-authored with the General an article on civil rights and national security for the *Yale Law Journal*.[1] This was during the time of the Cold War and at the height of the McCarthy period. I held the strong belief that civil rights should never be bent to accommodate national security concerns. The General did not agree. He carefully considered every issue I raised, but frequently weighed the values differently. He was not an ideologue and was willing to spend long hours debating the strengths and weakness of whatever arguments I raised. Although I never persuaded him to take the position I preferred, we did manage to carve out a mutually acceptable approach and I respected him enormously.

One of my responsibilities while working for him was to review the voluminous mail the General received from the public and then prepare answers when they were called for. No letter was insignificant; even letters from school children asking for help with a homework assignment on why they should study Latin! Each was to be answered and a position taken. Once, I asked the General why he devoted so much time to answering all these letters and his reply was typical. He said it was important to honor their correspondence because you never know what kinds of ideas will spring from the public. He was someone who was not afraid to take an idea and try it out. [2]

One day the General called me in and asked me to look into the case of a Carl Marzani. Marzani was a State Department official who had been found guilty of perjury when he denied he was a member of the Communit Party. Mrs. Marzani had written the General and asked him to sign a petition requesting her husband's parole. She had multiple sclerosis and was trying to care for their two children alone, and she desperately needed Carl's help at home.

After thoroughly researching the case I prepared a detailed memo outlining the circumstances surrounding it and whatever facts I could find on his status as a member of the Communist Party. When the General read my memo, he called and said, "Oh no, Mary, what I want to know are the facts surrounding his family situation and something about his wife's illness." So I made more inquiries.

Mrs. Marzani had represented her medical situation correctly and I duly reported this to the General. He never told me what he had decided. Much later while going through his files looking for something else I came across the Marzani file. I found that the General had sought the advice of several of his high-powered friends, David Bruce, John J. McCloy and General George Marshall. They counseled him against signing such a petition, but he disregarded their advice and signed it anyway. I never asked him why, but I am certain it was because he cared what happened to a fellow human being. He was never afraid of taking risks. I am told he always stood up for his people in the OSS when they came under attack, and he was doing that now in private practice.

I spent many weekends at the General's New York apartment working with him on one thing or another. Many times he would express regret at his present inactivity and he told me he felt powerless to effect national policy. Of course, I protested.

Many years later when I read about his career at the OSS, having experienced my own decompression from public life, I gained a deeper understanding of what an enormous letdown it must have been for him to just practice law. He had been at the center of world power, dealing directly with President Roosevelt, Winston Churchill and Joseph Stalin while he planned and executed many of the OSS-led operations.

When I knew him he was still a vigorous, imaginative and fearless man, but his glory days were over. I can understand how bereft and impotent he must have felt sitting in his law firm office when all he could do was rage against Acheson's cautious "panty waist" policies, or meet with the current military generals who were the ones active in various war fronts, or occasionally take on a special assignment in the Far East.

I first met the General's wife at a dinner party in their New York apartment. Ruth Donovan was a quiet and uncommunicative woman. The General had invited me to make a fourth and go with them to the theatre. A General Dean, who had been a prisoner of war in Korea for many months, was also there and the two of us made most of the conversation. The General had no gift for small talk, and clearly his wife was no better. I got the impression she gave the General very little emotional support. But I must admit I never really saw them together very often. Also, I cannot imagine what it must have been like to spend a life married to such a single-minded, preoccupied and dynamic man.

And their lives were filled with tragedy. His brother had been killed in a violent accident and they had lost their daughter, Elizabeth, the same way. When I knew him, his adored grandchild, Patricia, died at the age of six by accidentally drinking silver polish and his daughter in law, Mary, who was very attractive, outgoing and had acted as his hostess, committed suicide. I can't imagine how he bore all that and what it did to him, or to his wife, for that matter. No wonder he often asked what his life had really meant.

But he did go on, and continued to respond to requests. George Polk, a CBS correspondent had been murdered in Greece and the press had formed the Lippmann Committee to Defend George Polk. The committee had asked the General to represent them and help uncover who was responsible for Polk's death. The murder was deeply intertwined with Greek politics and the struggles against the communists. At that time the communists were rising up throughout Europe and trying to upset the status quo by defeating the more liberal social democratic parties. I spent several months on this assignment and produced a forty-page report for him. I never did find out what he did with it but, according to a recent book about the George Polk murder, the General sent only a much-abbreviated summary to the committee. [3]

When I was not working for the General, I did a lot of work for Lloyd McMahon, one of the top litigators in the firm. We worked on the Government's enemy property suit that was brought against General Aniline and Film Corporation. The company was believed to have been jointly owned by I.G. Farben and several Swiss banks. One of the banks, I.G. Chemie, was our client, and also had Washington counsel.

As far as I know, I.G. Chemie hired us to evaluate the strength, and weaknesses of the government's case. At one point the director general of I.G.Chemie, Herr Walter Germann, came to New York to talk with us about the case. We showed him our offices and then proudly pointed to the rows of open file cabinets in our documents room that contained the I.G. Chemie files. He made no comment.

When Lloyd and I went to Washington to meet again with Herr Germann and his Washington counsel, John Wilson, we realized what a faux pas we had made. Wilson brought us into his office and opened one of his desk drawers with a key from his pocket; then he took another key from his desk drawer before going to the file room where the I.G. Chemie case files were kept under lock and key. He pointed to the line of padlocked file cabinets and Herr Germann was duly impressed. He was very pleased to see his files were given such high security.

Lloyd and I stayed in Washington for a couple of days learning as much as we could about the background of the case. After we returned to New York, it became clear that we needed to go to Basel, Switzerland and look at the client's files at their company headquarters. We caused problems from the moment we arrived. We didn't want to spend two hours eating lunch the way the Swiss do and we asked permission from Herr Germann to work over the lunch hour. That caused a major crisis!

He wouldn't give us a key to the office so we could just go out for a quick bite and return. Instead he insisted that we must not be alone and there must a representative from his office with us at all times. We finally worked it out but for a while it seemed like a major international incident. The solution was that one of his "lady typewriters" was to be put in the office where we worked. After a day or so she came to us and said, "I am surely disturbing you. I will ask Herr Germann to give me another room." We told her she was not bothering us, but she insisted. Later we realized she was put there to spy on us and she felt uncomfortable about her role.

The bank staff was very nice to us, particularly after we had called all of them in and explained what we were doing and why we needed their help in identifying, xeroxing and refiling the various bank documents we were examining. I don't think they had ever been treated as a part of a team before, and they responded with warmth and enthusiasm.

Neither Lloyd nor I liked the Swiss very much. They were stiff, self-righteous and hypocritical. At the time my sister Betty and her husband, Jim O'Grady, a Foreign Service officer, were stationed in Basel and that made a world of difference to us. It was great being with them and it certainly provided a welcome relief from the uptight Swiss. Jim was Vice Counsel and had wonderful diplomatic skills. He and Betty were a good team. At that time, Foreign Service wives had an important role to play in their husband's work since very few women were professional Foreign Service officers.

Lloyd and I stayed in Basel for about two months before finishing up and coming home. We hadn't been back long before the U.S. Government served us with a subpoena and demanded we produce a second set of books for our client, I.G. Chemie.

David Schwartz, the bright young government lawyer in charge of the case, had done a thorough research job analyzing the company books and found they had cooked the books. There had been a considerable amount of post dating and rewriting of many of the entries. We weren't particularly surprised by the subpoena. It had been clear to us from the beginning that I.G.Farben and I.G Chemie had a history of obfuscating the facts and creating dummy corporations to make it difficult to trace their corporate history.

During our earlier analysis of the Farben documents we came across an intriguing memorandum on its strategic planning. The document was probably written in the mid thirties, when Farben was busy creating armaments for Nazi Germany. Farben was looking 100 years ahead and planning its manufacturing and marketing strategies to include China. It saw China as the largest potential market for its soap products and Farben developed a long-range strategy to create demand in this billion-population market. Its strategy was to conduct a public campaign in China that would stress cleanliness and personal hygiene as a value for the Chinese people.

One day, Joe Welch came into our office concerning a case his Boston firm, Hale and Dorr, was litigating in New York City. They needed New York co-counsel. Welch was famous for his representation of the Army during the 1952 McCarthy hearings when he lambasted Senator Mc-

Carthy for his demagoguery and bullying of senior army officials. Welch was outraged at McCarthy's irresponsible attacks on foreign service and army officers, calling them "pinkos and commies." Joe Welch then asked the rhetorical question that made him famous: "Senator, have you no shame?"

Welch deserved his reputation but, like most of us, had his Achilles heel. He would come into our office daily and talk with Lloyd about the motion we were preparing for his client. He always looked at me rather strangely even though I tried very hard to act and speak like a lawyer. Finally the day came for us to go to court. As the junior lawyer on the team, protocol demanded I carry Lloyd's bag, but it was heavy and Lloyd wouldn't let me carry it.

Welch and I took our seats in the back of the courtroom and Lloyd moved to one of the front tables where the other lawyers in charge of the case were seated. After a short while Welch turned to me and asked if I had ever gone to law school. I knew what was coming. I tried to deflect him by telling him not only had I gone to Yale Law School, but I also was managing editor of their *Law Journal* and had graduated COIF. But in his mind it was beyond the pale that I could be a practicing lawyer, so he just looked at me and said, "You must find that very useful in your work!"

My time at the Donovan firm was a wonderful and exciting experience. I loved the cases I worked on. But after five years I decided I should broaden my experience to make sure the legal world would fully accept me. I knew if I were ever going to reach my goal and be made a partner in any Wall Street firm, I would have to be a specialist in one branch of the law.

General Donovan agreed with me and told me about an opening at the New York office of the U.S. Antitrust Division and he offered to help. I always liked the policy end of law so I thought that specializing in antitrust would be interesting. I have often wondered if it was the General who had it in his mind that I should leave the firm, and managed to convey this to me without my realizing it.

After I left, I heard they told other women applicants that once they had hired a woman and it hadn't worked out. I knew the General liked my work but I was quite blind to the number of partners who rotated around him and were jealous of those who got too close. Unfortunately,

I made no effort to be tactful or get along, It didn't occur to me I needed to. So probably my self-perception was wrong. Also, I had fallen in love with one of the married lawyers in the firm and it's possible they knew this and decided to take some action. All along, I thought the decision to move was mine because I wanted to get more experience, so I took the General's advice and was hired in the New York office of the Antitrust Division.

Sadly, the last time I saw General Donovan was in 1957 when I visited him at Walter Reed Hospital where he had been diagnosed with arterial sclerotic atrophy of the brain. This was a degenerative disease that ultimately caused him to lose his mental capabilities and eventually, control over his physical movements. When I came into his room he recognized me immediately, but placed me in a different time and place. Nevertheless, he went back to a conversation we had had while I was still working for him concerning an emotional dilemma I was facing and he wanted to know how it came out. Despite his infirmities, he continued to have these flashes of memory and insight. It was amazing to me how that brilliant mind still worked! But sadly he knew he was dying. He said to his partner, George Leisure, "This is a hell of a way to die."

General William J. Donovan died February 8, 1959 and he was buried at Arlington Cemetery with full military honors, next to his granddaughter, Patricia. President Dwight D. Eisenhower delivered the eulogy at his funeral and said, "What a man! We have lost the last hero." [4]

Notes

1. Donovan, William J. and Jones, Mary Gardiner, "Program for a Democratic Counter Attack to Communist Penetration of Government Service," 58 *Yale Law Journal* 1211, (1948-49).

2. A good example of this was when the General was running the OSS. He had encountered a psychologist from Harvard University who had proposed to him a system he had devised to determine the espionage potential of OSS applicants. The General being the General said, "Fine, let's try it." A testing ground was then created at what was then the Congressional Club. It had been taken over by the OSS for the war period. Applicants were divided into small teams of three, two real applicants and one an OSS agent. Each team was given a particular assignment such as crossing a stream, for example, and an axe and a piece of rope as tools to accomplish the task. Just as the team got their bridge in place or at some point during the process, the OSS stooge would drop something or fall against the structure and the task had to be repeated. The goal was to observe who on the team took leadership, how each maintained his cool and how they resolved the problem before moving on. No one had tried this type of hands on experimentation before. But the General could see the potential and found the money to try it out. Apparently it was very successful.

3. Edmund Keeley, *The Salonika Bay Murder: Cold War Politics and the Polk Affair* (Princeton University Press, 1989. The book discusses my report and its handling in some detail, pp. 285-89.

4. *Wild Bill Donovan, op. cit.* p. 833.

Public Service Beckons

A month after I joined the New York field office of the Antitrust Division of the U.S. Department of Justice I received a pink slip saying I was fired. I couldn't imagine what had happened. It was January 1953 just before Dwight D. Eisenhower was sworn in as president, and I realized the incoming administration had probably reviewed the recent appointments and, assuming these were Democratic patronage jobs, fired us across the board. I immediately called General Donovan. I never heard anything more. So I just continued to work as if nothing had happened and in the space of two months, I was hired, fired, reactivated and started to work in my first public service law job.

In working for the government, an important asset is having experience because responsibility is thrown at you early. I was happy I had had my practical legal training in a law firm but now I was delighted to be able to spread my wings in government service. Our office consisted primarily of Jewish and Catholic lawyers who tended to stay within their own groups. I found myself gravitating towards the Jewish lawyers because they appeared more sensitive to professional women. Many had their foreign-born mothers and grandmothers still living with them and several of these women had had important status in their native country. For the first time I had the strong feeling these were people who liked and respected professional women. I felt insecure because I was a woman but I worked hard and got myself assigned to fascinating cases.

My first case was against IBM. The company was charged with monopolizing the tabulating machine card business, the precursors of the electronic data processing machines or computers. IBM refused to sell their punch card machines and insisted on leasing them. By prohibiting their customers from reselling IBM equipment, the company prevented the rise of a second hand market that could compete with them. IBM also had agreements with National Cash Register and International Telephone and Telegraph to stay out of each other's fields. Finally, IBM maintained a large patent portfolio in related business fields that it could use to keep other businesses from entering the field.

IBM was an all-encompassing corporate culture and it was fascinating to go through their files. They even had a corporate songbook with songs such as "Here's to Tom Watson Tried and True." Watson was the genius who founded IBM and he prided himself on claiming you would never find a pencil in any of his offices. IBM was a multi-national company and during World War II, the German Reich offered Watson a major honor. The managers of his German company, Dehomag, feared Hitler might retaliate against the company and they urged Watson to accept the honor and not antagonize him. But Watson was very clear about who he was, what he believed and what was at stake. He refused the 'honor'.

Despite Watson's strong personal ethics, however, there was little doubt in our minds that IBM had engaged in unfair trade practices by monopolizing the punch card business.

I found myself in my element when settlement negotiations began and during the discussions I developed a kind of third ear. I was able to listen to IBM's arguments and assess their importance to their regular business and then determine which of their arguments were overstatements and which made business sense. It was a fascinating challenge. We were lucky to have a top-flight law firm on the opposing side that played hardball but played fair.

I'm not convinced the provisions we bargained for succeeded in preventing IBM from continuing its dominant role in the industry. However, the negotiated settlement did prohibit them from continuing their lease-only policy, and we also prohibited them from continuing the "division of fields" agreements they had with NCR and IT & T, freeing those companies to compete with IBM and ensure that IBM did not exploit their dominant role.

The most significant result of our suit against IBM was Remington Rand's (Rem Rand) decision to take advantage of the suit and enter the electronic data processing industry. The existence of our complaint against IBM presented the opportune time for Rem Rand to introduce its UNIVAC system. IBM, with the government breathing down its neck, couldn't use its market power to stop Rem Rand from doing this.

With UNIVAC on the market, IBM's tabulating machines would soon become obsolete. IBM had to accelerate its move into this new field and the computer industry was born. The rest, as they say, is history.

When the IBM case was over, I attached myself to a pending international cartel case against the watch manufacturing companies in Switzerland and their American distributors. The government charged the Swiss companies with conspiracy and claimed the companies were restricting the manufacture of watches and watch parts in the United States and restraining U.S. imports and exports of both products. I thought the case would be fun, particularly given my attitude towards the Swiss.

I worked on the case for several years and watched my various bosses come and go. To our surprise, the Swiss decided not to settle and instead went to trial. As luck would have it, I was the only lawyer left who knew the case well enough to try it. Otherwise, I am certain that as a woman they never would have given me the responsibility of being in charge of a major antitrust litigation.

For the first time in my career as a lawyer I worked with another woman, two, in fact: Louise Florencourt from the Washington Antitrust Division and Magdalena Schoch, an expert on German law who was also familiar with Swiss law. The fourth member of my team was Carl Steinhouse, perhaps the most loyal and put upon, who, I learned later, had taken a lot of ribbing about working for a woman. Up until this time, I had problems keeping staff and never knew what I had done to alienate them, so I deeply appreciated Carl's loyalty. And I didn't ask what the problems were. Perhaps if I had been a man, my difficulties, whatever they were, would have been tolerated and I would have been regarded as eccentric or difficult or both. But as a woman, I had to be beyond reproach. And certainly they wouldn't have gone to the boss and asked to be removed.

It was only recently that I learned from Carl that the lawyers had agreed among themselves not to work for me! So, all my life I have believed that it was I who was at fault and in my naiveté it had never crossed my mind that I was the subject of my fellow lawyers' discrimination.

My relationships with my watch case staff were different. We worked well together. By this time I had started psychoanalysis and I suspect it helped me a lot. Also I was lucky that the judge assigned to the case, Judge John Cashin, liked women. He was not an intellectual but was very savvy. He had been a judge in Kingston, New York and was 60 when he was appointed to the federal bench.

At the time of the antitrust case Judge Cashin seemed overwhelmed but always maintained his savvy when sizing up witnesses and evaluating their testimony. The defense lawyers did not miss his obvious admiration for women and suddenly women were appearing in the courtroom as part of the defense teams.

It turned out that most of the defense firms had women lawyers but they were rarely allowed out of their firms' libraries. I hadn't paid any attention to this until one day I met Judge Cashin in the hall and he nudged me and said, "Do you see all those women lawyers appearing on the defense teams because you are on the case? That is what you have done. You've brought them all up here." But they were never permitted to utter a word in the courtroom and they just sat there.

There was another reason this fascinated me: I asked myself when had these women gotten their jobs? It was less than ten years since my vain search for a job in a major law firm and apparently law firms now were admitting women to their sacrosanct offices but they were not giving them visibility and certainly not in the courtroom!

In the midst of getting ready to try the Swiss watch case my psyche came apart. Among other things, I couldn't even make ordinary phone calls to the defense attorneys to arrange for various meetings. If my boss, in a most benign and non-threatening manner, would inquire about progress in the case, I would have a panic attack and start trembling. I knew something was terribly wrong. I had had disappointments and yearnings in my personal life but had accepted them as the pattern of my life. They certainly didn't cause me to question my emotional stability. But when I had difficulty carrying on with my professional life, I knew something was very wrong. So I started psychoanalysis to enable me to keep body and soul together, and was able to continue with my work.

The trial opened on November 14, 1960. We had originally named twenty-four defendants in our complaint and ten of them settled before the trial. So, we were four lawyers on the government side against a battalion of fourteen different law firms representing the remaining defendants. Jim Hayes from my old firm, Donovan Leisure, represented one of the defendants. He didn't like me and I didn't like him. However, Jim made his hostility to me so obvious that his fellow lawyers had to calm him down.

In January 1961, we went to Paris and took the depositions of various witnesses. In mid-February, we started the New York phase of the case. Our case was straightforward and didn't take very long to present. I put Magdalena Schoch on the witness stand to testify about some of the Swiss laws we intended to rely on. I didn't do much to qualify her except in a very general way because her training was in German law. Had I tried to show her knowledge about Swiss law, it would have looked as if we had scripted it beforehand. However, we were lucky. One of the defense lawyers who, as I suspected, had the traditional contempt for women lawyers, decided he was going to show up her ignorance. He asked all kinds of obscure questions about Swiss law which she answered in detail and he qualified her in a way I never could have. So much for stupid mistakes; and so much for prejudice against women!

The defendants opened their case in March 1961 with their first witness, a Swiss Supreme Court Judge who ponderously recited every conceivable Swiss law he said justified, authorized or mandated what the Swiss watch companies were doing. He was making patently exaggerated interpretations but this was really their only possible defense.

I sat through this watching Judge Cashin, who seemed to be totally intent on what the Swiss judge was saying. I knew the Judge was impressed by titles. He used to describe himself as a hayseed judge from upstate New York, and was always amazed he had become a federal judge.

When the Swiss judge's testimony was completed, it was mid-afternoon, so Judge Cashin adjourned my cross examination until the next morning. This gave me overnight to plan how to respond to his arrogant testimony. I was tempted to confine my cross examination to a few gimmicky questions about what the Swiss defendants had done that was required by Swiss criminal law. (I knew it wasn't.)

But I was concerned about Judge Cashin. I was afraid he had been impressed by the Swiss Supreme Court Judge's stature and testimony and might think we didn't have a case if I didn't try to shake the judge's interpretation of all the various civil laws he was testifying about. Good sense got the better of me and I decided I would never be a match for the Swiss judge's ability to stick to the testimony he had already given. I decided instead to go with a few questions where I knew I was on solid ground, and leave it at that.

The next morning I went to court, asked my few questions, and sat down. That confused the defense; they didn't expect that, and argued they weren't ready to proceed with their next witness. I was pleased when Judge Cashin ruled they had to proceed. Many days later I met Cashin in the hall and he said, "Thank goodness you didn't waste time cross examining that old windbag!" His savvy prevailed and I was relieved. I knew a judge could make your life difficult if he wanted to but Judge Cashin never did.

When Carl Steinhouse took over to argue against one part of the defendants' case, he was nervous. After all, none of us had ever tried a case before. The lawyers for the defense pounced on Carl and proceeded to make his life miserable by continually objecting to how he framed his questions. Judge Cashin adjourned the trial early, then pulled me aside and told me to get Carl in shape or do the cross examination myself. But the next morning, Carl was fine and the defendants stopped harassing him. Carl went on to be a first-rate trial lawyer and partner in the prestigious law firm of Jones Day in Cleveland, Ohio. Today, he is retired and writing fascinating books about the heroic acts of people like Raoul Wallenberg who rescued Jews during and after World War II.

The Swiss case ended May 17, 1961 and involved 8,000 pages of transcript and a total of 1,296 documents; 731 by the government and 565 by the defendants. A year and a half later, on December 20, 1962, the Judge handed down a 115-page decision in favor of the government. We won! So much for green trial lawyers. I loved it!

Despite the fact that we won the case, it wasn't over. A battle took place between the Justice and the State departments over the next steps to take. State was concerned the case was interfering with Swiss-American relations and wanted to settle the case on very modest terms. I was shocked to see one branch of our government intervene in such an important case involving the fate of the American watch industry that was important to our national defense.

Finally, the settlement was concluded. The negotiations took place in Washington D.C. but I was not a party to them. Nor was I invited—perhaps because I had strong views on what needed to be done to prevent the Swiss from dominating our industry; or, more probably, because I was a woman and couldn't possibly add anything to the Washington experts.

About this time I got into a bitter fight with my older sister, Ann. When my father died, twenty years earlier, my two sisters and I inherited our family home and sixteen acres in Cold Spring Harbor, where we had all grown up. We rented the house for a number of years and in the summer of 1959, when the renters moved out, my sister Betty and I were abroad, and Ann and her husband John just moved in. They declared the price they would pay and refused to discuss any other terms of the sale that my sister Betty and I thought were germane. As always, my mother sided with Ann because, as she put it, "poor Ann needed the property."

We finally gave in, gave up our claims to owning the road into our adjoining property (which was Ann's "service" road), instead of being a right of access, and agreed to the substantially below market price Ann and her husband had insisted on. In return, they agreed that if they resold any part of the property, they would share the proceeds with Betty and me.

During the Swiss watch trial, I drove out to Cold Spring Harbor to see Ann and was shocked to see two new houses built on the property we had 'sold' to her several years back. She had never lived up to her side of the agreement to share the proceeds of any sales of the property, and when I reminded her of our agreement, she said she had "forgotten" the clause. I said that didn't mean she did not have to live up to her agreement.

Again, mother sided with Ann, arguing that if I pressed our claim for reimbursement, Ann's marriage could be in jeopardy. Then she complained to Uncle Livy—unbeknownst to me—that I was starting family fights to harass Ann. Betty was abroad at the time, and felt helpless. She gave me a power of attorney and told me to act on her behalf. I knew this was traumatic for Betty, as it was for me. We both hated family fights, but I felt this was in important issue for me. Thanks largely to my analysis, I was able to stand up for myself, and with Betty's consent, I sued Ann for the amount she owed Betty and me. We quickly settled the case for $20,000, which was nowhere near the money she owed us, but I felt we'd had made our point. My object was not to recoup the money but to let Ann know she could not disregard her sisters' rights and interests.

Years later, when Uncle Livy died, in his will he left Ann the $20,000 she had paid to Betty and me in the settlement. I was very upset. It was if my uncle was striking back from the grave. Uncle Livy had always been a kind of substitute father and protector to me. Even as a teenager I remember him telling mother to lay off "the child" when, as a brand new driver of sixteen, I had overturned a friend's car with four of us inside. We had crawled out the window and, fortunately, none of us were hurt. Mother was furious, not because we might have been hurt, or I was careless, but because she had to pay for the damages.

I had always seen Livy as a tower of strength; not until much later did I realize how very dependent he was on mother. She obviously had succeeded in persuading him that my fight with Ann was baseless, and I never did have the opportunity to come back to it with him. Somehow I felt betrayed.

I worked on the Swiss watch case for five years, and after the trial ended, I thought it was time for a change. I loved litigating and I loved public service. For me there was no greater excitement than walking into a courtroom, rising when the judge walked in, and saying, "Ready for the United States Government." But, I was tiring of government service. I didn't feel I was growing anymore and I didn't feel I was learning from my colleagues. But aside from that, there were my career goals. I didn't see any further opportunity for me as an upwardly mobile attorney in the antitrust division and I wanted to get back into private practice. I thought that was my real legal career.

Now I had earned a reputation: I had tried an international cartel case and had won; the law firms in New York also knew about my work in the IBM case and I was a known factor with a lot to offer. So I began to look around for the opportunity.

Surprisingly, again I ran into the same degree of prejudice I had run into 12 years earlier. And this despite the fact I had five years in a large

New York firm, seven in the antitrust division and a major international cartel trial to my credit. Anyone else in my position would have walked into a partnership at almost any New York law firm. Fortunately, by this time I was able to handle this continuing prejudice because I had entered psychoanalysis and I was grateful for the psychological support that helped me keep going. No longer did I assume it was my fault if things didn't go well. I could appreciate the realities of the situation I found myself in, rather than see them in terms of my childhood experiences—real and imagined.

I finally was offered a job with Winthrop Stimson doing "blue-sky" work, primarily checking state securities law for new stock issues. I knew it would be terribly dull but I was convinced that if I took the job I would be able to show them what I could do.

During our last interview, we talked about salaries. They offered me the same salary I was making at the antitrust division and I told them it was equivalent to a salary cut since everyone knew that private law firms paid higher salaries than government. The interviewing partner looked straight at me and responded: "Well if you want to work for some uptown Jew firm..." My jaw dropped and I walked out of the interview, grateful I had heard that before I accepted their offer.

I was back on the street job-hunting again. As luck would have it, about this time I received a post card from the Wellesley Career Office that asked in effect, "Are you looking for a job? Can we help"? I quickly scrawled on the back of the card "I suppose you don't get any requests for lady lawyers?" I got a prompt call from the head of Wellesley's Career Office. She had received my scrawled note and responded, "No, we don't but we have Wellesley fathers and trustees who are lawyers so send me your resume and I'll see what I can do."

In a couple of weeks, I received a call from her saying, Simpson Thatcher, a large New York law firm, was looking for an antitrust litigator. She told me to call Dick West, a partner in the firm whose wife was a prominent member of Wellesley's board of trustees. I called Mr. West and made an appointment to see him. He told me his firm had just sent a large antitrust case over to Webster Sheffield, another well know New York law firm, who needed an antitrust litigator to handle the case because their senior litigator had just left the firm. He suggested I see the senior partner, Bethuel Webster, and I immediately made an appointment.

One of Beth Webster's first questions was about my age (I was forty) and then he muttered, "You don't look it." It seemed a funny comment but I didn't give it much thought. Only later did I learn he was grooming his son-in-law, Bill Hoagland, to take over the firm's antitrust work, but Bill hadn't yet been admitted to the New York Bar, and wasn't ready to take over the responsibility of a new antitrust case. Beth was probably concerned that I was that much senior in age to Bill.

It hadn't crossed my mind that this might be an impossible situation for me. I expected to be their antitrust partner and enjoy the partnership that every young lawyer is taught to believe is the goal of the profession. I passed the test of age and Webster introduced me to his partners and told me I was hired. Thus began the second of my private law firm experiences in New York. I was grateful that all this was happening while I was in analysis, because by this time I knew it would be essential if I were going to succeed in my new job.

Finding Myself through Analysis

The paralyzing anxieties I experienced while working at the antitrust division weren't the first emotional problems I had ever had, but this was the first time they interfered with me professionally. I knew I had to do something.

When I was in my teens, my mother took me to see her doctor because I appeared sad all the time. He said it was nothing to be concerned about, and typical of most adolescents' experiences. Then, while I was at Wellesley College, for no apparent reason, I would get what I called the "shakes." I went to the college health center and saw the head physician who knew me from hygiene class. She mentioned something about my being depressed. I didn't pay any attention to it and she, also a product of her times, didn't press the issue.

When I was in college, I thought that seeing a therapist was an admission of weakness. I had bought into the popular notion that willpower was the answer and words such as trauma, depression or counseling were relegated to abstract discussions in a psychology classroom. And I wasn't mature enough to see it for what it was: an early warning sign that my emotional and functional lives were in conflict.

Another episode happened while I was teaching at the George School. I was having frequent gastrointestinal spasms, and, again, mother took me to see her doctor. He found small differences in my white blood cell profile, and I assumed he didn't suspect there was any connection between my blood count aberrations and my emotional difficulties. My spasms disappeared after a while and I resumed my daily life and never gave it further thought.

By the time I was in the antitrust division, I thought I had perfected my ability to segment my life into two departments: functional and emotional. It was easier for me to ignore my feelings and just proceed to get on with my professional life. Unfortunately, I was born in a different time, and missed the opportunity, while I was still young and malleable, to bring these contradictions together and avoid the problems I faced later.

I had been working with the antitrust division for two years before I started to experience uncontrollable spasms of terror and emotional overreactions. I felt out of control. I would read a simple *Saturday Evening Post* story, for example, and break into tears or I would see a movie and it would become so real I couldn't tolerate the experience and had to leave the theatre.

I went to see the surgeon who had previously operated on a benign tumor in my left breast. He was a loving father-like figure who recommended I take a vacation, so I went to Malta to visit my sister, Betty. But that didn't calm me down. When I returned to the states, I sought the advice of another physician who gave me tranquilizers but these also failed.

Finally, out of desperation, I went to a law school friend who I knew was seeing a therapist and insisted he give me his name. My friend was seeing a psychoanalyst but had he been seeing a psychologist, I would have gone in that direction. The only sensible thing about my decision was that I respected my friend a lot; he was a very bright guy and it made sense to me that if he was going to someone whom he respected, that was good enough for me.

I remember my first session with Dr. Eugene Eisner as if it were yesterday. My appointment was for 4:10 pm and I was early. I waited in a little anteroom outside his office and promptly at 4:10 his office door opened and out walked a rather small slender man, with wavy brown hair, who in a gentle, sympathetic voice told me to come in. He pointed to the couch and like a compliant child, I lay down and waited for something to happen. I had no idea what to expect.

He took the lead and started asking me questions: for example, was I ambitious? I said, no, and explained it wasn't necessary for me to get to the top because everyone knew that, being a woman, I couldn't get there. Of course that was ridiculous but it was the rationale I relied on to handle the many rejections and obstacles I had experienced. He made no comment, asked some other questions and just listened. At the end of the 50-minute session, he said to me, "I will see you tomorrow at 3:20 pm." Being dutiful, and without asking any questions, I turned up the next day promptly at 3:20. And promptly at 3:20, once again he emerged from his office, beckoned me to the couch and again I complied. Thus began my six years, five days a week intense psychoanalysis with Eugene Eisner.[1]

During those daily sessions, Eisner made little comment. Gene, as I later learned to call him, was a product of the Freudian tradition. He had been trained both at the Menninger Clinic in Kansas, and at the William Alanson White Institute in New York. The Institute followed the theories of Harry Stack Sullivan who believed that individuals should be seen as a part of their environment. Gene admired him deeply and agreed with Sullivan that a patient's social environment was as important as their sexuality.

As far as the non-participating role of a therapist, Gene was very much a product of the Freudian tradition. But he was more tempered and less rigid, even going so far as to send his patients post cards from his various vacations, which Freudian therapists wouldn't do; as a rule they wanted to keep the doctor-patient relationship strictly impersonal. Later in my therapy, I felt comfortable enough to respond to Gene's invitation to call on him and his wife, Margaret, during their summer vacation at the Orchard Inn in Provincetown, Massachusetts, hardly a common practice with most analysts.

During the analytic sessions, Gene remained mostly silent and this infuriated me. I would rail about this and he always replied the same way: "If *I* were to ask you a question, it will point *you* in the direction you think *I* want you to go. I don't know whether that is the direction you want to go or not." He believed his intervention would be too controlling. I would go silent and didn't know what to say next. My silences were excruciating to me. Much later, I finally realized that a lot of my silence was resistance to opening up my life and that was something only I could overcome. Sometimes we had two-hour sessions; for some reason that helped me break my silences.

When I started analysis, I was 38 years old and still living in New York with my mother and two roommates; the lease on our apartment had a six month cancellation clause. I had insisted on that because my life always felt temporary: being single was not a permanent state and real life was just around the corner. I never did feel entitled to have a life of my own because I never felt I was worth much. My pursuit of a successful legal career was something apart from mother's expectations, and she was the touchstone of what was appropriate and right. Even though I refused to conform to her ideas, I had internalized her standards. I find it amazing that I had managed to survive these contradictions as long as I did.

I found analysis incredibly painful. I was always anxious about my sessions with Gene. I would have to drag myself there, and I dreaded it the entire time. I never did go in with the feeling of "Oh, I'm so glad I am here, I want to tell you something." There wasn't anything I wanted to tell Gene, I only wanted to hide. But somehow I kept on going. It was particularly difficult for me because of my legal training. A stream of consciousness is a major factor in analysis but that is not how my mind works. I go from Point A to Point B, and proceed from one to the other only after it has been carefully thought through ahead of time. At one point I remember Gene asking me whether he was going too fast. I said, "I don't know where you are going so I don't have any sense whether it's fast or slow!" I don't think in all my years of analysis I ever did "freely associate" or understand any of the process. Nevertheless, I got through it.

That first year was hell! I never did like talking about myself and I certainly didn't like having my carefully constructed beliefs and survival techniques torn away. I felt bereft and remember saying to Gene, "If you take that rationale away from me, I am nothing, nothing." Every night I would come home, eat supper and lie on the floor listening to music trying to pound the music—and the feeling it evoked—into my soul. But I persevered and kept going.

Gene used sarcasm as a technique to peel away the protective layers I had constructed and to pry me loose from my deep and rigid preconceptions. I would describe my family in terms of how they gave us the best: skating lessons, private schools, etc. And, of course, I talked a lot about my relationship to mother, how controlling she was, and how desperate I was for her approval. I also talked about my efforts to get her to love me. I remember telling Gene about the time I wanted to give her a mink jacket that she fancied but was afraid to give it as a present from me alone. I tried to persuade my sisters to be part of the gift, even though I was paying for it because I was convinced mother would get more pleasure from the jacket if it came from the three of us. They refused but I went ahead anyway. Gene referred to my efforts to buy mother's affection as the Jones Benevolent Society I was trying to run.

He also referred to Fraulein, our German governess, as the maid, which made me very angry since we all regarded Fraulein as a member of the family. Now I realize, however, what Gene was trying to do was to help me see that the one person who gave me the love I craved was an outsider, not a parent, and that my anger at mother's rejection of me was justified. Growing up, I always felt like two people, one good, the other bad, and I was never able to reconcile the two. He wanted me to come to terms with my anger over my sense of rejection and to stop always feeling so guilty and "bad."

Regardless of the difficulties of analysis, the experience of coming first with someone for a full 50-minute hour was wonderful. One day, I came into the anteroom of Gene's office and saw another patient who thought it was her hour. When Gene came out of his office I said, "Oh, I'll be happy to come back." Firmly but gently, he said, "No, Mary, this is your hour." For that hour, in my doctor's office, I was the most important focus of his attention. Some of the sessions went better than others but in general it was a difficult experience. Most of us who have gone through analysis talk about how wonderful it is, but looking at it objectively, we're talking about the ultimate results and not about the painful process where we have to explore feelings we would much rather hide.

Understanding my family and my reactions to them was grist for the analytic mill. I had to unravel how these conflicting emotions had contributed to my paralyzing anxiety and dread and had blocked me from functioning as a professional. That was really the crux of psychoanalysis for me—to bring these two powerful dynamics into balance: my emotional sense of myself based on what I perceived was my mother's view of me and my intellectual understanding of myself. The conflict was paralyzing me. I couldn't continue to feel socially inadequate and inferior and deny my intellectual achievements because they did not conform to my mother's view of the role of women.

Hearing myself trying to convince Gene how much mother really did try to do what was best for me, while also expressing how much I hated the world she reflected, finally helped me stop trying to live the lie that her life represented to me. Gradually, I began to accept that my values, though different, were equally valid and that to act them out was not only acceptable, but, in fact, essential if I was to shed my anger and feelings of guilt and become my real authentic self.

Analysis helped me to look at myself differently, accept what I always knew about myself deep down inside, and understand what had made me so angry. I always knew that mother was not a loving person, but I couldn't accept that perspective of her. In the process of analysis, I tried to be myself, started to express real feelings to my family and act out my new insights. I'm certain my analysis was almost as difficult for them as it was for me.

When I started analysis, my sister, Betty and her husband, Jim, were living abroad. Both of them were very supportive of me during this difficult time, but I am certain psychoanalysis was as much a mystery to them as it had been to me. I knew it was painful for Betty that I had so little memory of the things we had shared as children, and her feelings about me were always conflicted. On the one hand, I was the four-year-old brat always trying to assert herself and steal the limelight, while she, on the other, remained more passive and accepting

Another side to our relationship was Betty's description of herself as a mother hen. I always wanted to do whatever Betty wanted. In analysis, this changed. I no longer wanted to be "mother henned." I was trying to live for myself and not see myself solely in the eyes of another.

My relationship with Ann was more complex. Growing up, I had always been profoundly jealous of her and saw her as my mother's favorite—the pretty, blue-eyed, obedient, and successful child. Ann married at twenty-one and spent her entire life in Cold Spring Harbor taking care of her family.

Like my mother, Ann was always distressed that "poor Mary" had never married. Late in life, and despite all the emotional baggage of fights and jealousy, Ann and I did become close. When my mother died, somehow all my hostility towards Ann disappeared but I don't know how much of this I can attribute to analysis.

Several years later, when two of Ann's children reached their twenties, they came to live with me: the first was Abby, her only daughter, and later her third son, Charlie. I hadn't talked to Ann about their moving in, and I am sure it was hard on her. In our later years, when we were able to talk about it, I told her I regretted I'd never thought to talk it over with her. She said she had finally come to terms with it.

I'm certain that if Ann had had the right encouragement she might have tried to resolve many of her own inner conflicts. I remember her once saying to me, "I just want to understand who I am. Am I Ann Crooker, mother, Ann Crooker, wife, or just Ann Crooker?" She did try counseling once with someone in her Catholic church but it didn't work out so she didn't stay with it. But I do believe she had some appreciation of what analysis had done for me.

Looking back, I find it strange that I never talked much with Gene about my relationship to my father or to my Uncle Livy. I certainly talked about my two sisters. But my preoccupation was with my relationship to my mother, who neither understood my analysis nor wanted to try. One evening when I was going out, I told her I had an appointment to have a Rorschach ink blot test. After I explained that a Rorschach test was designed to determine a patient's various psychological associations with people and situations, she sat bolt upright in bed, fixed me with her eyes and said, "Now Mary, if that doctor thinks you're crazy then we have to do something about it." Now I see it as laughable. But at the time it came across as one more example of her inability to see me as a competent person capable of making my own decisions and living my own life.

In the winter of 1958, my mother left for her yearly Florida vacation and I continued to turn up every day at Gene's office. I was functioning in the antitrust division but was having difficulty holding on to my staff. They would ask to be transferred and I never knew what I was doing that drove them away. Gradually as my analysis progressed, I began to change and slowly I began to build a loyal and competent staff. Since I was in and out of the office at odd hours of the day I decided I had to tell my boss, Dick O'Donnell, what I was doing. I had been afraid to tell him but when I did I was shocked at his response. He said, "If my father had offered me a choice of a college education or analysis I would have chosen analysis." So much for trying to imagine what others might think!

There were several early breakthroughs. When I was about eight or ten, I would play out a wonderful fantasy. I imagined a log cabin sitting along the roadside that sold beautiful flowers and plants. In that fantasy, I created people on the porch who were beautifully dressed in deep red velvet gowns with decorative gold braiding. But all of them had blank faces. They were mannequins! My withdrawal from seeing people must have started when I was very young.

One spring day, about three years into analysis, I was walking across 96th Street on my way to the subway when, for the first time, I actually noticed that fathers were walking their daughters to school, or waiting with them for the school bus or just going to work. Before that I had never really seen people. Now, for the first time in my life, I was noticing that people had real faces, and they were acting like real people. As strange as it seems, it was an eye-opener for me.

A second major breakthrough came a year or so later. I always disliked New Year's Eve "celebrations." They seemed artificial, and I didn't like the pseudo-gaiety and feeling alone in a crowd. So I did what I had frequently done on New Year's Eve, and went to a movie by myself. I debated between seeing a comedy or a story about an orphan boy, Truffaut's "400 Blows." I decided on "400 Blows." Predictably, when I came out of the movie, I was totally depressed and felt extremely sorry for myself. Walking home alone along Madison Avenue, I suddenly realized "You're doing it to yourself, Mary, you deliberately chose a movie that would depress you." With a burst of insight, I recognized I was in control of my actions and of how I chose to deal with life. This revelation alone freed me from some of the helplessness and hopelessness I had lived with for too long.

Gene loved Americana. Looking back on our sessions together, I realize he spent a lot of time on my family origins. He was fascinated by my family background because it stretched back to the late 1600s. But I realize now it was more than that. He wanted me to come to terms with my heritage and he gave me my first real appreciation of my family.

He helped me accept that I came from a long line of people who had made important contributions and I could be proud of that. I talked a lot about the Joneses and the Gardiners and particularly about my suffragist Aunt Rosalie. I never knew much about mother's forbears. The Joneses were much more alive to me because we lived among them on Long Island.

Mother had always been critical of the Joneses, so I am particularly grateful to Gene for helping me recognize who I was in relation to that side of my family. And my acceptance of my background contributed immeasurably to my development as a total person.

Two years into analysis, my mother and I came to a peaceful parting of the ways. I had changed jobs from the antitrust division to the Webster Sheffield firm and when she came home from Florida in early May 1960, she said, "Your uncle thinks that the trouble with you is living with me. What do you think?" I thought to myself, "Dear God, if I don't say yes now, I never will." I knew my only hope was to agree so I struggled to reply and finally blurted out, "Yes, I think that's true." Certainly, two years earlier, I would have been full of denials because I would have been afraid to hurt her. I would have indulged my compulsion to take care of her and be nice to her in my usual attempt to get her to love me. Now I knew I had to save myself. Mother was astonished, but to her credit made immediate plans to get her own apartment; she got in touch with Fraulein and the two of them moved in together.

Uncharacteristically, Gene got involved. He recommended I get in touch with Bess Bernard, an interior decorator he knew to help me furnish my apartment. By now, my roommates were married, so once mother moved out I had the apartment to myself. Bess was very good. She never dictated any particular style to me but instead helped guide me towards finding out what I liked. With her skillful promptings, I realized I had my own tastes and a firm preference in both color and furniture style: blue and English antiques.

Previously, if left to my own devices, I probably would have purchased unfinished furniture because I was always thinking I wasn't worth any more than that and my real life was in the future. Gene told me that furniture was often a device families used to control people, so if mother offered to leave me any of the furniture, I should make it clear that I liked it (if I did) but I might someday sell it or give it away.

In fact, mother did make several suggestions, and I made the appropriate reply. When the dust finally settled all that was left in the apartment was the bedroom furniture I had as a child and the spinet piano I had bought several years earlier. After I finished redecorating, I had an incredible sense of peace and beauty and pride of ownership.

Now, at forty, for the first time I had a sense of my own life. I had been on my own and supported myself since I graduated from college, but now I realized I owned my life, and my external and internal lives were beginning to merge.

It is interesting for me to realize that I came to know Gene so well despite his silent, non-intervening style. I learned to know him in bits and pieces over that long, six-year period. I believe he was trying to let me see parts of him in my sheltered life. He was an interesting man from a cultured, Jewish family that had emigrated from Hungary. Both his mother and his sister were musicians and he had trained to be a concert pianist. He never continued on that path, however, and instead chose medicine. He had two children, both of whom I met over the years and have remained in touch with to this day. They have become close friends. Gene loved the opera and collected abstract paintings and stood in direct stark contrast to my mother's outspoken prejudices about Jewish people.

Growing up, I don't remember books or literary magazines around the house. When my mother did read, it was mostly novels from Wormrath's, the local neighborhood lending library. Getting to know Gene helped me validate myself and accept my own interests in music, especially opera and the intellectual world. I am sure it was his influence that led me to take piano lessons again. After some false starts, I finally located a teacher who taught me how to make music and not just play the notes; he, too, has remained a dear friend.

Basically, what I learned from analysis was that I could grow and become a full human being once I shed the myths and lies I had constructed about my role in the family. I learned I didn't have to accept their concept of marriage or what they perceived as a woman's role. Before analysis, I dealt with that by ignoring those social aspects of my life that created a barrier between my family and me; instead, I focused on my intellectual life, where they couldn't play a part.

My way of coping was to accept mother's assessment of me, assume it was accurate and do everything I could to prove I was lovable: give her an expensive mink coat, or in the summer invite her to live in the upper part of my small country house when she had rented her own place in Cold Spring Harbor. I had internalized her expectations of me and tried desperately to live with the conflict between her view of what a proper woman should be—married, subservient and non-assertive—and what my growing sense of self demanded of me.

After six years in analysis, these conflicts gradually eased. I worked very hard to find the 'me' that had been smothered by mother's expectations of me. I also learned that an important part of me was my family origins. Now I can embrace that rich heritage without guilt or thinking it somehow makes me special or better than anyone else.

But most important of all, I learned I was valuable as a human being and slowly, painfully, I developed self-esteem. I know these are words carelessly bandied about, but I learned how essential it was to respect oneself in order to fully function as a human being. I learned I didn't have to be married to be a lovable person capable of loving and being loved.

I regret that I didn't come to peace with my mother while she was alive. After I had been appointed to the Federal Trade Commission she tried very hard to ask questions about what I was doing; but no sooner would I begin to tell her than she would be off on another subject. Unfortunately, mother was self-centered and incapable of being genuinely interested in another person. It took me a long time to accept that. With the help of analysis, I learned to step back and see her more clearly: not for what I wanted her to be but for what she was—a tragic figure, who, for whatever reason, was incapable of love.

And I am sorry I was never able to come to grips with my father. My friends tell me I talked a lot about him when I was a child but I don't remember any of that. For me, my father barely existed. My growth as a woman was colored by my lack of a cherishing relationship with my father. I realize, too, how strongly I was influenced by the other male figure in my life, Livy; hard working, successful, and homosexual.

I never totally mastered the familial influences that dominated my early life, and from time to time those demons still rear their ugly heads. Life for me is an ongoing process of uncovering the various ways I allowed myself to be dominated by my mother. It is a continuing struggle and one where I have needed help to see that influence for what it was. I realize life is an ongoing journey, and I have not hesitated to seek further professional help when I experienced periods of paralyzing doubt and anxiety.

But going into analysis gave me my life. It enabled me to flower and survive.

Notes

1. In those days, psychoanalysts charged $50.00 an hour. That came to about $1000 a month for me. My government health insurance Aetna paid 50 percent of it. Luckily, I had had a small inheritance from my Uncle Arthur of $20,000 that went to pay for the part of my analysis not covered by insurance.

Reentering the Private Sector and President Lyndon Johnson Calls

I was still in analysis when I went to work as an antitrust litigator for Webster Sheffield. It was a small firm of about thirty-six lawyers with a practice that consisted mostly of estates work, a large number of public oriented clients, several foundations and an assortment of other clients. The largest cases they had were price fixing complaints against the electric utility companies and that is what prompted them to hire me. Without the help of analysis, however, I doubt I would have been able to take over such a large assignment.

I was in charge of the electric utility litigation and had two male colleagues, Bill Hoagland and Don Elliot, who reported directly to me. I felt we were working pretty well together, but I became aware that I was doing something to alienate other colleagues in the firm. I had come to Webster Sheffield with prestige and respect, yet somehow I managed to dissipate that and was never quite sure why. Although I was the lead attorney, I developed a childish and unrealistic jealousy of Bill and Don that created all kinds of difficulties for me as we worked on the electric equipment cases. Fortunately, I was still in analysis and, through my work with Gene, I began to see that in my working relationships I had a tendency to place my colleagues and myself in a family sibling constellation in which I was vying for approval from a good father figure, who in this situation was the senior partner, Beth Webster. My siblings became Bill and Don. Gradually, as I came to understand these demons, I felt more secure and was able to more realistically exert my authority.

As the first year progressed, I took several steps in my personal life, small to some but large to me. I took my first independent travel and went on vacation by myself! Up until this time, I usually did the safe thing and spent vacations with my sister, Betty, in whatever foreign country she and Jim were living in at the time. Their State Department postings were always exotic and visiting them satisfied my desire to travel.

My new independence took me in new directions and it worked out well. In the 1960s I took my vacations at Chanterwood, a lovely camp-like resort in the woods near Tanglewood, Massachusetts that was accessible only by a narrow mile-long dirt road. The cabins I stayed in first were primitive and didn't have their own bathroom so I had to use the shower and toilet in a nearby cabin. We ate together in a big lodge with board games and a library, and went canoeing on the lake. I learned to reach out and made good friends.

Other ventures were not as successful. After finding Chanterwood, I decided to branch out and go to the Salzburg Music Festival in Austria. The music was wonderful but I still tended to isolate myself. On one day's excursion into the surrounding countryside, I was the only person on the bus who didn't have someone sitting next to them. I'm convinced my inner emotional turmoil sent the silent message, "Stay away!" On another trip to hear opera in Munich, I resolved to go down to the bar and meet people. I talked with a nice friendly man who was also traveling alone but then couldn't follow through when he suggested we meet after the opera and have a drink.

I spent most of my four years at Webster Sheffield working on the electrical equipment price fixing cases. We represented a few of the fifty electric utilities that had brought separate suits against nineteen electric equipment manufacturers involved in nineteen different product lines.

Faced with this complicated multi-litigation, the courts made a landmark decision. They compelled the plaintiffs in each of the product categories to join together and said that a single law firm must be in charge of each product line case. Then they directed the chosen firm to work with the other plaintiffs' lawyers and collaborate with them in the final presentation. There was a lot of legal maneuvering between the plaintiff and defendant law firms, who were seeking information about the various transactions involving each other, as well as the circumstances surrounding the price the utilities paid for the various products they purchased.

As we took part in this multi-law firm litigation it shed some light on how law was practiced by some of the country's top law firms and we were able to experience first hand how their buddy system worked. The utility cases involved the various firm's senior partners, all of whom knew each other. Also, both the plaintiff and defendant companies were corporate giants and their CEOs were often old friends who were members of the same clubs and associations.

One of the New York firms that represented a defendant we were suing served a motion on our clients to produce a large number of documents. We regarded their motion as irrelevant and unnecessary to the case and were convinced the firm brought the motion just to embarrass and harass our client. We took their motion to Beth Webster, who agreed with our analysis of the motion. After discussing a variety of strategies we might use, Beth decided to just pick up the phone and call the senior partner in the other law firm. The conversation went something like this: "Good morning ... Tom. We just received a motion that was filed by some young lawyers in your firm. The motion has really no basis in fact and goes beyond what anyone would regard as a reasonable document." Beth gave him some examples of what was being asked for and then he said, "This kind of conduct really won't do." The senior partner agreed. The motion was withdrawn and the case moved on!

Lawyers working on these complex cases traveled in packs. When a deposition was to be taken in Miami all the plaintiffs' lawyers involved in the case set out for Miami, participated in their client's deposition and then came home: Always together!

On one occasion, we were scheduled to meet in Washington D.C. for a meeting and have lunch at the National Press Club. When I arrived, the Maitre D' stepped forward and said I couldn't go in because the Press Club didn't allow women in their dining rooms. Everyone was upset and much conversation ensued. Finally, the club capitulated, put a screen around our table and then led me into the dining room through the kitchen to our table that was now safely hidden from public view! I'm ashamed to admit that I didn't have enough gumption or self-respect to simply walk out and say I'd rejoin them after lunch. But I was too eager to please and anxious not to call attention to the fact that I was a woman, screen or no screen.

After the cases were mostly concluded, I was assigned to work for another partner in the firm, Ethan Hitchcock. But Ethan would never let me go to court or let me see clients on my own. It was clear that I needed to be made partner before that could happen, but Ethan still couldn't understand why being a partner was so important to me. I tried to explain I had done my apprenticeship and didn't like younger lawyers breathing down my neck.

Unfortunately, I never was able to persuade Beth Webster to make me partner. Now I'm convinced it was because he wanted his son in law, Bill Hoagland, to head the firm's antitrust litigation section as soon as he passed the bar, and the firm was too small to sustain two partners, both specialized in antitrust. I was getting increasingly upset over not making partner and began to think about changing careers. Finally I went to talk to Manley Fleischman, another partner in the firm, and asked him about the possibility of my changing careers and getting a non-legal job. He said he was sure that would not be a problem and that if I really wanted to leave, he would help me.

But life is serendipitous. About this time, Worth Rowley, a former boss of mine at the antitrust division of the Justice Department, called and told me of a vacancy on the Federal Trade Commission. He said President Lyndon B. Johnson was looking for a woman and with my antitrust background I had the right qualifications; so, if I were interested he would submit my name. I told him to go ahead and I began to pursue the possibility.

Federal Trade Commissioners are presidential appointees and the law specifies that of the five Commission members, no more than three can come from the same political party. The vacancy was for a Republican spot and with my family background, everyone assumed I was a Republican. Also I had worked for two prominent Republican law firms and that placed me squarely in the business-oriented private sector.

When I first moved back to New York, in a feeble attempt to make friends, I had joined a Republican club in my neighborhood but I don't remember ever being involved in any club activities. I had never registered for a political party before because I hadn't wanted to be committed to anything, but after learning about the opening I formally registered as a Republican.

I suspect I was more conservative then and at best, I was non-political. However, I don't remember ever voting for a Republican president; I had voted for Franklin Roosevelt, Harry Truman and Adlai Stevenson. I was a strong civil rights advocate during law school, but I was more of an internationalist concerned with the UN Declaration of Human Rights. In the fifties, my concerns shifted to the national civil rights scene spurred on mostly by Joseph McCarthy's witch-hunt against so–called communists. Also, I was a loner and was never active in a group; I think, unknowingly, that provided me with a protective cloak and outside my professional circle people didn't know me very well. Taken all together, this helped to give me the necessary Republican coloration.

I was ready for a change. The idea of a federal appointment was very appealing and I certainly wanted to be appointed, so I began to look into what I could do to maximize my chances. I called John Lindsay, the Republican Congressman who, at the time, represented New York's upper east side. I had known John since my early childhood on Long Island and we were in law school together but I hadn't seen much of him in the past few years. He was the only political person I knew, but what I didn't realize was that by calling him for advice, I was asking for a political favor. He called me back immediately and said he would be happy to help.

Congressman Lindsay asked if I had talked with Esther Peterson, President Johnson's consumer representative. I said, no, and he urged me to call her immediately. I did, and Esther was very positive, asked me several questions, and said she would be happy to help. And so the process began in earnest. John then told me he had spoken to Beth Webster, and I should talk with him and line up my two state Republican senators, Herbert Lehman and Jacob Javits. I would need their endorsement to get the appointment and Beth, of course, knew them both.

I was beginning to learn the political ways of Washington! I decided I needed to talk to Manley Fleischmann, who I knew was a Democrat, and ask him if he had any advice about what else I should do. Manley said he knew the economist, Eliot Janeway, and Janeway was acting as a type of advance man for President Johnson, screening candidates for federal jobs. As Manley put it "he owes me one." I was very lucky.

Both John Lindsay and Manley Fleishman were willing to spend political chits on my behalf. So I went to see Eliot Janeway and I still remember the interview. For about five or ten minutes we made small talk about what I had done, etc; then he leaned back in his chair and, looking directly at me, said, "You strike me as a complete political innocent, I will support you." That was my qualification for the job! Actually, it made sense because I was to fill a Republican spot in a Democratic administration.

By now I thought I should not leave any stone unturned, so I called Lloyd Cutler. Lloyd was an old friend of my Uncle Livy and his former assistant when Livy was running the Lend Lease office in North Africa during World War II. Lloyd, a well-regarded and prominent Democratic lawyer in Washington, graciously said he would help. I asked if I should do anything else and he thought I should leave it alone.

But I did call Marcus Hollabaugh and Ephraim Jacobs, two former colleagues I had known in the Washington office of the antitrust division who counseled me on how best to approach Senator Javits. Marc got very excited and filled me full of details on Javits's antitrust activities on the Hill. When Ephraim walked me to the elevator, he said in his slow southern drawl, "Mary, you probably won't have more than five minutes with Javits, if that;" hardly time to discuss the antitrust legislation Marc had outlined for me!

For the first time in my life being a woman was an advantage. President Johnson wanted to appoint able women. For example, he called his Secretary of Agriculture, Orville Freeman, and told him he wanted women appointed to top jobs in that department. Later when I looked at my file in the LBJ library in Austin, I found out I was the only woman candidate they even considered.

I was in my New York office when I received a call from Johnson's appointment secretary, Ralph Dungan, who asked me if I would come down to see him. I went to Washington immediately and saw Dungan in the Executive Office that was then housed in the old State Department building. I thought we had a great interview. I was very relaxed because it never occurred to me I would get the appointment. I remember asking him what he looked for in a candidate. He said the first thing he looked for was to learn who was in whose pocket. Then we talked about the difficulties in getting a good spread of candidates. He was disturbed because his reach of candidates was largely limited to the eastern seaboard; he had grown up in New Jersey and had gone to school in the East.

Then he looked at me and said, "Take you, for example. The other evening I was at a cocktail party in Washington and ran into Lloyd Cutler. I asked him about you and he gave me his impressions. I couldn't have done that kind of informal checking about someone from the South, the Midwest or the West."

He also told me LBJ had wanted someone from the business world to balance the other FTC Commissioners whose careers had been mostly in government before they were appointed. His staff had contacted people in business, but found their background too specialized and several business school professors had turned them down. They considered me because of my background practicing law with private New York law firms representing business clients.

After the interview, I walked down to the FTC to look around the building. I ended up standing in the front hall gallery looking at the portraits of all the former and present Commissioners. Never in my wildest imagination did I think there was a chance I would be appointed and that one day my picture would hang in that gallery.

I had my Washington interviews in June 1964, and by August I still hadn't heard anything. I assumed nothing was going to happen and I headed off for my usual vacation at Chanterwood in Massachusetts. As I drove my little red Triumph into the courtyard, the proprietor came running out shouting, "Mary, Mary, the White House called, they want to see you in Washington right away." I immediately turned my Triumph around and headed back to New York City. My apartment had been closed for the vacation but I stayed there overnight. The next morning I went out to get a quick breakfast, and when I returned to the apartment to get properly dressed before catching my plane to Washington I found I had locked myself out! Fortunately, at least I had my purse with me and since time was critical, I had to go to the airport as I was—dressed in a little sundress.

When I arrived in Washington I went directly to the White House and sat outside the Oval Office looking like something the cat had dragged in. After some time, Johnson's Chief of Staff came out and with profuse apologies said the President was tied up and would I come back at 2 p.m. I heaved a sigh of relief, raced out, bought a dress, shoes and accessories at Garfinkle's, had my hair done at Arden's and was back in the White House at 2 p.m. transformed into what I hoped was a proper FTC candidate.

Eventually, President Johnson came out, greeted me, and then took me into the Oval Office. He seated me on a small sofa, and he sat in a chair opposite the sofa so he could look squarely at me. I was awe-struck! And I remember being surprised that he was so tall. He was extremely gracious, gentle, kind and immediately put me at ease. LBJ was in the middle of his presidential campaign against Barry Goldwater and he told me that appointing me as the first woman Federal Trade Commissioner would be seen as sheer politics. He wanted me to know this wasn't his intention and he said, "My mother was a very intelligent woman, my wife is a very intelligent woman and I have two daughters who are equally intelligent. We are wasting women's talents because we haven't appreciated the contributions women can make," and he wanted it to stop. He was sincere and convincing and I wanted to cheer. The president then said he was going to send my name up to the Senate and I would hear from him soon. I was on cloud nine. I couldn't believe it!

I went back to my law firm in New York City and immediately prepared to make my farewells. But the weeks went by and I didn't hear a word. There was no indication that my name had ever been sent forward to the Senate. There was a small item in the *New York Times* reporting a rumor that I was to be appointed, but there was nothing else. Finally I called Ralph Dungan to inquire. I told him my firm was planning farewell parties and I was beginning to worry. He said something had come up and I should be hearing soon. After several weeks, I got one of those "Would it be convenient to come to the White House?" calls. I can't imagine it ever being inconvenient to come to the White House!

I went down to Washington, worrying the entire way about what was happening. Once again I was ushered into the Oval Office. The president told me that after the news item had appeared in the *New York Times,* the White House had received several letters opposing my nomination. This was intimidating but I remained silent. He read me one of those letters that said I was an antitrust "persecutor" who wouldn't listen to opposing arguments. I found out later the letter had been written by Stanley Temko, whose firm had represented the Benrus Watch Company, one of the defendants in the Swiss Watch case.

LBJ said he wanted me to hear what people were saying about me and then he looked me squarely in the eye and said he always wanted it said of me, that as a commissioner, "She always listened, she was always accessible." Then he added, "You may be the only contact people have with their government and I want it to be a positive experience." He sent my name to the Senate that very day.

President Johnson gave me the feeling of deep sincerity and love of government. This was borne out much later by my experience with him after he withdrew his candidacy for reelection and invited me to luncheon at "his" library when I was giving a speech in Austin. I am convinced that the side he presented to me on both these occasions was an important and very real part of him.

Of course, I talked over the opportunity at the Federal Trade Commission with Gene, who was quite negative about my appointment. He was conservative and concerned about the transitory nature of politics. But I also think he was impressed by the firms I had been part of in New York City and I doubt he ever appreciated what it was like to be a woman in that arena. By now I recognized that I had grown through my years in therapy. Even though I was totally devoted to Gene and appreciated that he had given me my life, I was also proud that by now, in spite of his reservations, I was able to pursue this opportunity and go to Washington to become a Federal Trade Commissioner..

I was also aware that by leaving Webster Sheffield and starting my career as a government public servant I was beginning a whole new chapter in my life. My intensive analysis was winding down and I felt ready for this new challenge. But I also felt I needed some transition. For the first few months I was in Washington I would drive to New York on weekends so I could continue my sessions with Gene. After I had been a Federal Trade Commissioner for a few months, we terminated our relationship and both of us felt good about it.

I was on my own.

Commissioner Honey, the Federal Trade Commission

"Commissioner Honey" was the sobriquet former Commissioner Lowell Mason gave me when he introduced himself to me in my new office at the Federal Trade Commission. I thought it was charming and seemed to epitomize my life as a professional and a woman. I always had difficulty accepting these dual identities—both my analysis and my appointment as an FTC Commissioner helped me bring these two disparate selves together. It also marked a dramatic shift in my life—not only was it a new job responsibility, it also meant a new place to live. Since my earliest days at the OSS I had always associated Washington with freedom and independence and now I was back, at the pinnacle of everything I could hope for.

By the time the President sent my name to the Senate for confirmation, Congress had adjourned for the election campaign and I was given a recess appointment. While I waited for my hearing, I sought the advice of two of the FTC Commissioners who suggested I make a courtesy call on both the Majority and Minority heads of the Commerce Committee, which I did. [1]

The committee gave me several questions they intended to ask so I was well prepared when I finally appeared before them in February 1965. An FTC Commissioner is a lowly appointment in the total scheme of things, and, at that time, not every presidential appointment was as politicized as it is today. Moreover, this was when the woman's movement was beginning to gain widespread public attention. Betty Friedan's

Feminine Mystique had just been published. Ralph Nader's automobile safety battle with General Motors was dominating the headlines. No one was going to go hard on the Federal Trade Commission's first woman appointee at this particular moment in our nation's history.

Members of the committee sat on a semi-circle dias and I sat in front of them at the witness table. Senator Jacob Javits (Republican, New York) sat next to me and made a brief statement in support of my nomination.[2] After his statement he left and I was next. Some of the committee members' questions were concerned with my "honest" intentions to serve out a full seven-year term. They asked if I saw my role as commissioner as an advocate or champion of any particular interest group, and they asked how I felt about strict regulation. I was even questioned about whether I smoked—I didn't—and to what extent I favored making Commission actions public—I did.

One exchange we had was amusing: one senator stated his belief that the Commission "needed an independent woman ... down there to do as the distinguished Senior Senator from Maine (Margaret Chase Smith) always does, digging those French heels in and saying 'Look, we are going to get this report out in this committee or I am going to make the report myself!' "

To which I replied: "I will sharpen my heels, Senator." My appointment went through the committee easily but the hearing underscored for me the reality of our basic system of government and impressed upon me the seriousness of the responsibilities I was undertaking.

The Federal Trade Commission is a regulatory agency that was established in 1914 and is one of the many agencies created by Congress that uniquely reflects our country's separation of powers. The president appoints the commissioners but no more than three are allowed to be members of the same political party. The Senate then approves these appointments and has final say over who will be a commissioner. The House, however, has the power over Commission actions by exercising its budget and oversight responsibilities. This makes commissioners acutely sensitive to the interests of the various House committee members and how they feel about Commission policy. When I was appointed, the House was concerned about the Commission's policies relating to mergers and consumer protection.

Congress passes the FTC budget every year and this reflects the bottom line of congressional approval or disapproval of the Commission's performance. What was interesting for me to learn was that the Commission couldn't send its budget to the Hill before it got the president's approval. Once, during a Commission meeting, when I protested that our budget request was too small, Rand Dixon, the chair of the Commission, said: "Mary, you don't have to stand up to the president's eyeballing you and telling you, you are asking for too much money!" Commissioners are able to maintain their independence because they serve a seven-year term and cannot be fired except for dereliction of duty. Still, many commissioners want to be reappointed and this makes them sensitive to what the president wants.

The Sherman Antitrust Act was passed in 1890 and prohibited undue concentration of economic power and unfair competitive practices. Twenty-four years later the Federal Trade Commission Act was passed to prohibit unfair and deceptive marketing practices and promote competition. The FTC also has specific jurisdiction over corporate mergers and shares this role with the Department of Justice. It also monitors print, radio and TV advertisements as part of its jurisdiction over unfair and deceptive practices, and has the power to make industry-wide studies and issue binding rules. Administering these laws was my major responsibility as a commissioner.

My life at the Commission was one I never would have imagined—I found myself professionally. I reveled in the autonomy and responsibility I had, with enough power to do proactive things. I was in an environment where the FTC could make a real difference in the lives of consumers. I found that with my FTC title, I had no problem calling up any leader in business, academia or think tank if I thought it was relevant to an issue we had under investigation; or I could walk into the offices of any CEO of any company confident they would see me. I also found out that I could attend any affair and without qualm introduce myself at receptions, lunches, dinners and even breakfasts. My title gave me the self-confidence I had lacked in my social life in New York. I loved it!

When I joined the FTC, it was the 1960s, a time of great tumult; fundamental changes were going on in our nation's economy, as well as in our political attitudes. The strains of this social and political upheaval were evident even at the FTC.

The marketplace had changed from local owner/consumer businesses based on personal relationships, to an impersonal national marketplace. Small businesses were being gobbled up by giant producers and sellers. Also, almost all consumer goods were promoted by national advertisers and they were sold by national chains that had little or no ties to the local community.

Automation and technology created new standardized products; synthetic fibers like nylon and polyester were developed, and new and more complicated kitchen appliances were designed. Many products were unique and complicated with unfamiliar properties that made "do-it-yourself repairs" difficult. This forced consumers to be dependent on the producing corporation for information about the product, its proper use, and its servicing.

The FTC saw this as a challenge to design consumer-friendly rules. A classic example was the clothing labeling regulation that forced clothing manufacturers to disclose on the product the contents of its fabric materials, as well as how to care for it.

The 1960s also created a climate of social change that saw increased consumer awareness of deceptive market practices, and new consumer demands for product information. In 1962, President Kennedy issued the first charter of consumer rights and two years later, President Johnson appointed Esther Peterson as the first Special Assistant for Consumer Affairs. In 1966, Ralph Nader's explosive book, *Unsafe at Any Speed*, created a new safety ethic in the marketplace, and, as a result of Nader's book, the safety risk shifted from the consumer to the manufacturers, who became responsible for the safety of their products. [3]

This was the business and social climate when I joined the FTC. I didn't realize it at the time, but the FTC would soon become the focus for change that was sweeping the country to address consumer discontent. As the first woman FTC commissioner, I began to receive invitations to speak to various consumer organizations, even though I knew little about the consumer movement.

Speaking to groups from around the country, I learned first hand about consumer discontent. They were eager to know about market place deceptions, and how to recognize and protect themselves from them. It also became clear to me that as FTC commissioners, we had to listen to consumers and hear their concerns.

I was an eager learner. It wasn't long before I became knowledgeable about the movement, and sensitized to consumers' needs in the marketplace. Almost immediately, I was plunged into all aspects of the Commission's consumer work, and I devoted my early speeches primarily to the Commission's current practice of protecting consumers by regulating business practices that were harmful to them.

After every speech I would come back to the Commission with the names of organizations and people who were interested in our actions. I managed to drum up my courage, and as the newest commissioner, I started a campaign to persuade the other commissioners to include the consumer in the occasional hearings we held on business-wide practices.

Furthermore, I said we needed to address our educational materials directly to the consumer, and not just to business. I suggested we create a consumer mailing list so we could send them notices and information about our actions, and hopefully this would encourage the consumer to write the Commission about their experiences in the market place. Before this time, the FTC had little consumer contact. Instead they had relied on complaints they received in the mail from industry about practices of other industry members (usually their competitors) who allegedly had violated the law.

Gradually the staff began to understand how consumers saw their problems, and they began to look for industry practices that had the greatest adverse impact on consumers, as well as practices that were unfair to other businesses. When I suggested to the other commissioners that we invite consumers to our hearings, my fellow commissioner, John Reilly said, "Oh, Mary, not the ladies." He was thinking of the cartoon-type female reporter who at times would turn up at Commission hearings to talk about a market practice of concern to her readers. I replied: "John, if that's who comes, so be it." The Commission agreed.

I remember the first hearing to which consumers were invited. The topic was the environmental impact of detergents on consumer health. A smart, good-looking young woman was testifying for one of the environmental groups when Rand Dixon, our Chair—a good old boy from Tennessee—savvy, shrewd and with an eye for the ladies—leaned over and whispered to me "if that's who consumers send, by all means let's have more of them!"

Rand was old fashioned but I have a sneaking suspicion he was rather pleased to see a woman on the FTC. Early in my tenure I went to him and said, "Rand, I need a wife." He looked at me, smiled and asked what I wanted. I told him a second secretary to help me with the personal side of my life. He understood immediately, enlarged my budget, and I hired another secretary.

Each commissioner was assigned three lawyers. Since I was a lawyer, I thought I didn't need lawyers as much as I needed the experience and knowledge of other disciplines. So, I hired two lawyers and an economist. Later I substituted a marketing expert for one of the two lawyers. I thought I needed some one who specialized in marketing techniques, since so much of what the Commission does deals with advertising and marketing practices. The first person I hired for marketing was Murray Silverman, a professor from San Francisco State University. Murray was experienced, knowledgeable and exactly what I needed to help me deal with advertising and sales deceptions. I directed him to spend time with the Commission staff and help them understand the ways that individual industries develop their marketing and advertising practices. The staff found his expertise invaluable, and soon they began to hire their own marketing consultants.

Relatively late in my term, I hired a business school graduate as an adviser to help me become a better manager, a skill too few lawyers have. I began an intensive effort to get the other commissioners, and the staff, to engage in strategic planning rather than continue to let staff propose complaints that happened to come to their attention. My goal was to have the Commission set policy objectives each year, and then have the staff implement them and report the results back to us.[4] This left staff free to exercise their best judgment on case selection based on overall policies laid down by the Commission as to areas we wanted to have priority. However, the other commissioners were a stumbling block. As lawyers, they were more comfortable reacting to staff proposals about which complaints they should initiate. The staff was also opposed to strategic planning because they didn't want to see their autonomy diluted in case selection.

Sadly, during my term we never did resolve the question of how best to set priorities for the Commission. However, we did succeed in getting the staff to create an information database on various industries, the overall economy, and specific consumer demographics that ultimately helped them in planning their work. I believe that my efforts, along with those of my staff, did leave a legacy of policy planning that continues within the various Bureaus of the FTC.

In 1967, Ralph Nader published his report on the Federal Trade Commission. It was devastating. It criticized the Commission for its slowness in responding to consumer concerns and condemned the staff for its continued attention to frivolous outdated problems that were of little concern to consumers.[5] I had to agree that Nader was right in criticizing the staff for its lack of imagination and zeal in carrying out its consumer mission. This was why I had tried to introduce policy planning at the Commission in order to curb this power of staff to select cases.

When I was appointed to the FTC, there was little doubt that cronyism prevailed. When the Commission was first created in 1914, it was said to be the dumping ground for political favorites of the Tennessee Senator who was then chair of the Commerce Committee. I don't know if the story is true. But I do know that at the reception after my swearing in, practically every other staff person who came up and introduced him or herself to me said, "I am so and so. I am from Tennessee."

All the various bureau directors that our chair, Rand Dixon, appointed were from Tennessee, as he was, and clearly there was a lot of cronyism among the top staff. Rand also had the demeaning belief that if you hired the brightest out of law school they wouldn't stay around very long. Instead he focused on the middle range student he hoped would stay at the Commission. This was the climate within the Commission when the consumer movement was heating up.

Still, as a hard working, consumer-minded commissioner, I was upset at Nader's critical report. I knew that some of us had been working hard to change the Commission from its pro-business orientation to a more dynamic, consumer-oriented federal agency. But I also found Nader's blast useful because it pushed me to be more insistent on the changes I wanted to make.

His report became my ammunition to prod some of the other commissioners to pay more attention to consumer interests. It also enabled me to point out that if we didn't do such and such, the advocates, the press and even Congressional committee members would be all over us.

The report was also useful in galvanizing public opinion. It helped form a vocal and sophisticated consumer constituency, and it also helped develop a responsive audience in Congress. Later it became "politically correct" to ask consumer- oriented questions when we had our oversight hearings on the Hill.

When Richard M. Nixon was elected president in 1968, one of his first acts after his election was to appoint Casper Weinberger, a California public service TV moderator, and consumer feature writer on the *Los Angeles Times*, as Chair of the Federal Trade Commission. Cap, as everyone called him, focused his energies on getting rid of many of the Commission's deadwood staff but he only stayed six months; before being appointed director of the Executive Office of Management and Budget.

President Nixon next appointed Miles Kirkpatrick, a lawyer in an old line Philadelphia law firm and author of the American Bar Association's equally critical report on the FTC. Kirkpatrick brought in top-flight staff to head the major bureaus within the Commission that brought new life to the agency where it was badly needed.

The chair of a federal agency can make an enormous difference for good or ill and in Miles' case it was definitely for the good. He wanted to make the Commission proactive. He agreed with the direction that Commissioner Philip Elman and I were going as we worked to move the Commission away from just educating businesses about their FTC responsibilities and toward more affirmative consumer protection activities.

Under Miles' leadership, and with the enthusiastic support of Commissioners Elman, James Nicholson and me, the FTC developed a series of new enforcement tools. This was the heyday of a pro-active FTC, working to find effective ways of protecting consumers. Before Miles, the Commission had relied largely on cease and desist orders to protect consumers that really only said to an advertiser or scam artist, who deceived the public, stop doing what you were doing.

One of our new enforcement tools was a "cooling off" rule requiring door-to-door sales people to give the consumer a few days to reconsider their purchase. This rule gave consumers time to reflect on whether or not they really wanted the product. This remedy proved highly effective in diminishing the hard sales tactics used by door-to-door sellers against vulnerable seniors and inner city consumers.

Another important FTC regulation dealt with installment contracts. Before this rule, consumers who purchased goods on the installment plan weren't able to protect themselves if the product was defective or was different from what the retailer had represented it to be. A third party could purchase the installment contract and be free of any such consumer claims. The Commission ordered that even if an installment contract was sold to a third party, the consumer's claims must still be honored. The Commission's new rule deprived fraudulent sellers of a major tool they had been exploiting to avoid consumer claims against them.

Under the Kirkpatrick Commission, the process of inviting consumers to participate in Commission hearings, and listening to what they had to say was greatly accelerated. Bob Pitofsky, the new director of the Bureau of Consumer Protection, came to the Commission with both private practice and an academic background. He was very proactive. He sought out and encouraged consumers to give input on Commission actions. Their participation proved to be invaluable.

Two consumers, Geoff Cowan and Eileen Adams, proposed the concept of substantiated advertising. This required advertisers to have proof of the various claims they were making before their ad appeared in the marketplace. The idea created an effective way to prevent exaggerated or false claims, and gave lawyers a tool to make sure their clients' claims were defensible.

A group of George Washington University Law School students, SOUP, Students Opposed to Unfair Practices, petitioned the Commission to intervene as a party in the FTC's false advertising complaint against Campbell Soup. SOUP wanted to intervene to ensure that there would be an effective sanction against Campbell Soup if it were found to have violated the law as charged. They requested what came to be known as a "corrective advertising" sanction against Campbell Soup that would require Campbell to publish new advertisements saying their former ads were false, and had misrepresented the quality of the soup. The Commission (over my dissent) didn't permit SOUP to intervene in the case, but we unanimously adopted their creative sanction proposal.

The concept of corrective advertising was new. We had always complained that, typically, after a Commission decision was sustained in court, the advertisement had long since disappeared from the marketplace. The only sanction the Commission had ever used was an order for the company to cease and desist from future false advertising claims. Now, with corrective advertising in the Commission's quiver, a company would have to think twice about a deceptive ad because their public image would be damaged if they had to publish the fact that their former ad had been deceptive. I don't know how often corrective advertising has been used by the Commission but the power does exist and it's an important FTC remedy.

I disagreed adamantly with the Commission's decision not to permit SOUP to intervene. But the Commission stuck to its position that it represented the public interest, and, therefore, didn't need consumers to intervene to argue that point of view. To me, one of the Commission's problems has been that as good lawyers, commissioners and staff naturally want to win their cases. To avoid court challenges by business, we would ask ourselves whether the complaint was over reaching, was the remedy too strong or were we interpreting the law too broadly? Because consumers weren't parties to our complaint and couldn't appeal our decisions, we didn't have to ask ourselves the reverse questions: was the remedy strong enough, would it protect the consumer in the marketplace or were we interpreting the law too narrowly? To my mind, this also made the Commission too ready to compromise in settlement talks because there was no one actively presenting the consumer point of view.

Obviously, my personal passion was with consumer issues, but my work at the Commission wasn't exclusively that. Like the other commissioners, I received many invitations to speak to the business community. They were mostly interested in the Commission's work that directly affected their business and I was invited to talk about consumer and antitrust issues that might affect them.

My goal was to help them understand how the consumer movement was good for business and how a consumer's concern should be viewed as an early warning signal from the market place. In my speeches, I could be a crusader. I was convinced that it was in business' own interests to respond to consumer demands and I was convinced they could do that and still meet their profit making goals.

Many of the topics we dealt with at the FTC involved important value and policy issues. For example one question was raised about whether it was appropriate for the Commission to publish news of their investigations of various business practices involving health and safety issues before a complaint was filed. We debated whether the public should be alerted as early as possible to the possible personal risk that was involved if they purchased a particular product under investigation, or whether the public's right to protection should be subservient to the possible damage to a corporation's image if our investigation didn't pan out. I believed then, and believe now, that consumers should have as much early warning as possible about the health and safety of a particular product they want to purchase. After much discussion, we agreed the consumers' right to know should take precedence over an industry's concern about the impact our investigation might have on their business.

Another difficult issue was whether it was fair, under the Flammable Fabrics Act, for consumers to be charged more for infant wear that was fire proof (as was the industry practice) than for infant wear that could burst into flames? Some argued that consumer choice should be paramount. In my opinion, presenting low-income consumers with a choice between buying a fireproof product for their children or buying the same product at a cheaper price that could catch fire was an unconscionable choice to have to make. My view did not prevail.

I was always mindful of President Johnson's advice to me to be seen as someone who listened to people and was concerned about their problems. This came back to me when I would get calls from consumers about problems unrelated to the FTC.

I remember one case in particular. It was that of an elderly gentleman in Big Gulch, West Virginia who was having problems with the Washington D.C. Social Security office. Apparently he had received what he thought was the usual run around when he called that office for help. So I called the Social Security office to find out what the problem was. They knew him well and had been grappling with his requests for several years.

Unfortunately, there was nothing that could be done. His problem was with the law not with the Social Security Department's implementation. I was upset. I wanted to help him and didn't want to write one more bureaucratic letter to him saying his government couldn't help. I talked it over with my staff to see if we could find some way to make him understand he had been heard but the law was not on his side.

One of my staff suggested I call him rather than write. I thought that was brilliant. I called him. I'm certain it was the first time that someone in Big Gulch, West Virginia had received a phone call from a Washington government agency. He was delighted and I continue to hope he is still talking about the government official who called him on the telephone to discuss his problem!

The Commission had its lighter moments. I wrote the majority opinion in a proceeding where I said the Commission had a duty to provide independent legal counsel to any defendant who was sued by the Commission and who couldn't afford to hire an attorney. My decision was distributed over the national wire services and picked up by several local newspapers. I began to receive calls from across the country from people who wanted the FTC to provide them with a lawyer. The message they gleaned from the news was, "If you need a lawyer, call Commissioner Jones."

Another day one of my attorneys, Sam Rozell came into my office waving a green sheet summary of a proposed Commission action. "Commissioner, I think you should abstain from this matter." These non-controversial green sheet matters were circulated, without Commission discussion, for automatic approval unless a commissioner put it on the agenda for discussion.

Sam had spotted this because it involved my cousin, Bobbie Gardiner. Bobbie had gotten himself involved with some outfit that was scheming to sell genealogies and using one of the Gardiner family crests in its literature. We were being asked to agree to a proposed settlement that had been worked out with the parties. Sam was right and I did abstain. But I was fascinated that my staff knew so much about my family connections. It would never have occurred to me to look up the backgrounds and family histories of my various bosses.

Sitting on the FTC was always intellectually and emotionally stimulating, interesting and challenging. It was a high point in my life.

Notes

1. A description of that confirmation process appears in Mary Gardiner Jones, "The Golden Age of the Federal Trade Commission, Innovation and Creativity in the '60s and '70s (II)," 1985, *Antitrust Law and Economics Review*, pp. 1-56.

2. Hearing before the Committee on Commerce, United States Senate, 89th Congress, First Session on Nomination of Mary Gardiner Jones, Federal Trade Commission, Feb. 18, 1965, pp 1-15. Other statements of support were submitted in writing to the committee by Attorney General Robert Kennedy, Republican Congressman John Lindsay and former Commissioner Lowell Mason.

3. Nader, Ralph, *Unsafe At Any Speed* (PB, 1966).

4. In those days, the commissioners took very little initiative in the selection of cases. Staff would monitor TV ads and mergers and identify law violations. Sometimes Congress would affect priorities by passing legislation in the credit field, or with respect to packaging of products. We couldn't ignore these laws and therefore assigned special staff to monitor practices prohibited by the new laws. Studies by our Bureau of Economics sometimes generated Commission actions. Some leads to possible deceptions and other law violations going on in the market place came from complaints that reached us by mail. But all of this case selection was essentially ad hoc. The Commission did not have any strategic plan of what industries played crucial roles in our economy or what marketing practices were most injurious to consumers or to the healthy operation of the market.

5. Examples cited by Nader were a deceptive advertisement by a nursery in a small town on Long Island for Christmas chrysanthemums and a series of cases involving failures to disclose the foreign origin of products. These were hardly issues of great moment to consumers who understood better than the Commission the globalization of the manufacture of most products in those days.

The Washington Life: Politics, Parties and the Commission

My life as a Federal Trade Commissioner in Washington proved more extensive than simply my actual work on the Commission. I had bought a house in Washington and I began to reach out and give dinner parties as well as go to the occasional reception for new or departing Commission members. To the extent I thought appropriate, I also got involved with some of the political issues riling the Washington community.

I enjoyed it all and found the social life in Washington more congenial than that in New York. If I went to a party in New York and someone asked me what I did and I'd say I was a lawyer, it was a conversation stopper! In Washington if I did nothing at all, *that* would have been a conversational dead end. New York parties were more formal affairs and careful attention was paid to make certain there were an equal number of men and women. Being single, this always presented a problem. In Washington it was completely different, you could invite uneven numbers of men and women and no one cared. Also in New York, parties were usually built around all lawyers or all advertising folk or some such pattern. In Washington, that wasn't the case. I found that most parties had wonderful mixtures of people from government, academia, freelance writers, press people, etc. The mix was stimulating.

At the beginning of my term, and after President Johnson's landslide victory in 1964, John Reilly, a fellow commissioner, and I were invited to a White House dinner for new appointees. I had been told that White House affairs ran like clockwork: cocktails at six and dinner promptly at six thirty.

I thought it was safe to drink one martini during the short cocktail hour but, as fate would have it, it was the night of a crisis in one of the Central American countries, and dinner was delayed for an hour. So while the president was doing whatever he had to do, a second martini came around and I accepted it while we made small talk with our fellow appointees.

Finally, dinner was announced, but first we went through the receiving line. After having our pictures taken with President and Mrs. Johnson, we finally sat down to dinner about 9 p.m. We were seated at small round tables of ten, set with beautiful White House dinner porcelain and two or three elegant glasses for different kinds of wines. Of course we drank them. After dinner the guests mingled and suddenly I found myself next to the president. All my small talk immediately went out of my head. After all, you can't exactly ask the president of the United States how he likes his new home or what he thinks about the Vietnam war! Somehow I managed to get through it, making some conversation or other, and happily the president soon moved on to another group. John Reilly finally came reeling over to me and suggested it was time to go home. The martinis and wine had their inevitable effect and we reeled out together, having had an incredible evening.

The only other White House affair I was invited to was during LBJ's inaugural festivities. It was a tea at the Smithsonian and I went over thinking there would be just a few select people there. Instead, there were thousands, mostly women. Muriel Humphrey, the Vice President's wife, presided. It was lovely to shake her hand but I learned one Washington truism; you quickly get cut down to size.

But I loved the Washington life, modest as it was for somebody at my level in the pecking order. Even as a former commissioner, I am still entitled to be called Honorable for the rest of my life, but I've never used that title. To me the perks were more important. I received rare free tickets to the Julliard String Quartet at the Library of Congress and was entitled, despite my Republican affiliation, to get tickets to all the LBJ inaugural events. I took advantage of that, invited some close friends to dinner and together we went on to one of the balls. Another awesome experience!

Receptions in Washington are endemic. They are given by the major consumer organizations and by innumerable trade associations and business groups. I felt it kind of obligatory to attend; after all, I was a public servant and I felt advocate, business and other groups had a right to be able to meet informally with their government officials. But the experience is heady, everyone being polite and sometimes even effusive—typically the business groups more than the consumer advocates. The trick is to keep one's sense of proportion, rely on one's inner integrity and discipline and know that the system itself—both the courts and the press—has its own built in checks and balances to curb unfairness and bias should it creep into one's decisions.

Politics is mother's milk in Washington. I didn't participate very much, but there were occasions when I found it helpful to do a little politicking. In 1967, John Reilly told us he had decided to resign as commissioner and move on to other things. He was uncertain about the date and Rand Dixon said, "Well, John, it doesn't make any difference what date you select, because the day you resign the president will appoint Mac Henderson to succeed you." Mac was General Counsel of the Commission and drank heavily. He was also lazy and seldom made any contribution to the few Commission discussions he chose to attend. In my mind, he would have been an absolute disaster. Both Phil Elman and I were appalled. Mac came from Texas and had a good paper record. Unless you knew his actual performance at the Commission, you could easily be fooled.

Phil did what he could among his Democratic friends on the Hill and I decided the only thing I could do was write the president a letter and express my opinion on the qualifications we needed in a new commissioner. Obviously, I didn't mention Mac Henderson by name. Instead, I wrote about the need for a young commissioner from a private practice background and preferably one who came from outside Washington. I never did receive a reply but I think I may have received an acknowledgment from John Macy, Director of the Civil Service Commission.

On December 10—I remember the date because it was my birthday— I received a phone call from the White House, once again asking, would it be convenient to come to the White House? I couldn't imagine what was going on. I had had no real contact with the president since he interviewed me for my appointment. I knew I was his so–called Republican appointee and aside from my tipsy White House dinner, there had been no other contact. In fact, our independent status as commissioners would have made such contacts questionable.

So I went to the White House wondering if I had done something wrong and they were about to ask for my resignation. Once again I found myself waiting in the antechamber to the Oval Office. Soon the door opened and the president came out and said, "Oh Mary, come in, I am sorry I have kept you waiting," He then proceeded to tell me he had just appointed Jim Nicholson to fill John Reilly's place and said, "Jim comes from Indiana, is in his early 40s and doesn't know much about antitrust. I want you to take him under your wing and show him the ropes."

I was dumbfounded! Then he told me he didn't really know Nicholson's politics (probably untrue) but assured me Jim was against discrimination. This was an important issue, as the Commission had a case pending against real estate companies in Washington who were alleged to be violating FTC law. The companies had refused to sell or rent to African Americans, and had failed to disclose this in their advertising. The commissioners had split 3–2 in favor of bringing this case and the president was telling me, in his way, we still had our third vote.

In the larger scheme of things, I don't suppose the president should have taken time to follow the Commission actions in such detail. But it was clear LBJ knew everything about the FTC's activities, including the ongoing differences I frequently had with Phil Elman. The president said he would take care of Phil if they continued. He was amazing!

Then he apologized and said he had to cut our meeting short because his Secretary of State, Dean Rusk, was waiting to see him and he also had to go to the rehearsal for his daughter's wedding. I was on cloud nine and open mouthed that the president of the United States should take time out of his busy schedule to see one of his commissioners. It was his way of saying thank you for my intervention, though he never did mention it.

Actually, the Commission's investigation of the D.C. real estate industry was the only time in my nine years as a commissioner that I dabbled in politics on the Hill. One of Rand Dixon's arguments against bringing the case was that we would be interfering with the housing discrimination legislation being debated in Congress. Our action might give some representatives an excuse not to push for a legislative solution.

His argument had some force with me because we knew that legislation could be more effective in stopping outrageous discrimination practices, and would be more effective than just a Commission's cease and desist order. All an order could do was direct specific defendants to stop future discrimination. Legislation would outlaw these practices across the nation.

I decided to call Senator Jacob Javits' office and ask for an appointment. I explained the issue to the senator and asked if he thought action by the Commission would be helpful or harmful to the passage of the pending legislation. Javits thought about this for about a minute then turned and said, "The Commission has a reputation for slowness. Go ahead but don't be in any hurry to press the case." I assumed he believed he could use our prospective action to his advantage in pushing to get the law through. Eventually the housing legislation did pass and we withdrew our complaint.

The only other time I ran headlong into politics on the Commission was during the Nixon presidency. My term on the Commission spanned the first five years of his term because LBJ had reappointed me after my initial two-year appointment. I put my hat in the ring to be named chair, though I knew my Republican credentials were meager. It was well known that I was a Republican in name only, but I felt strongly I should try for the appointment or I might regret it later. Needless to say, I was not surprised when President Nixon appointed Casper Weinberger as chair, who was then followed by Miles Kirkpatrick. It was not long before Nixon realized his mistake.

Miles had brought in a very activist staff, and was bringing several large merger cases that did not please the Republicans. I heard the Administration tried to get Miles to resign by offering him a judgeship. Miles promptly turned it down. I was in Palm Beach over Christmas that year visiting my mother and was invited to a cocktail party. When I got there I found myself dragged off into another room where I was introduced to Elmer Bopst, the Chairman of the Board of Warner Lambert who immediately started talking about the merger case we had pending against his company.

I squelched that by explaining I couldn't discuss a pending case. He quickly changed the subject and then asked me about my career and had I ever considered going on the bench. I told him that I hadn't considered it, but might do so after my term expired. That ended that conversation.

When I got back to Washington I went to Miles and asked his advice about whether I should put my conversation with Warner Lambert's chairman on the record. Miles' sense was that Bopst would deny the conversation. There had been no witnesses and it would be my word against his.

Since I had pushed to be Commission chair after the Republicans had won the election, Miles felt people might assume I was being a sorehead and just trying to get back at the Administration. That made sense to me. I was never quite sure it would have done any good to put it on the record. It probably only would have led to my being disqualified to sit on the Warner Lambert merger case when it came before the Commission. I didn't want that to happen so I let it go. However, I have always wondered just how many other people had had similar experiences, and also kept quiet for their own reasons.

The years 1964 through 1973, the years of my tenure on the Commission, were tumultuous times for the country. Martin Luther King Jr. was murdered in 1968, and riots broke out in several big cities across the nation including Washington D.C. Around eleven p.m., the first evening of the riots, my old friend from OSS days, Harold Lewis, called me at home. He was now back at Howard University and he was obviously very upset. He said "Mary, there is a curfew on. No black person can go out on the streets and I have a student who has been picked up and is in jail. Could you go down and find her?" I went.

I was not familiar with criminal cases so I wandered around the various courtrooms thinking she might be in one of these courtrooms waiting for trial. Judge Harold Green who was presiding over the arraignments of the rioters, saw me and sent his clerk out to see if he could be of help. It was about one a.m. and I saw several senior partners from major D.C. law firms looking for their young lawyers, clerks or messengers, who also had been picked up during the riots. They looked just as bewildered as I felt but at least we were trying to do what we could to cope with a difficult situation.

Judge Green's clerk was very helpful. He explained that a criminal defendant would be in the "tombs," not in the courtroom, and he volunteered to go down and look for her. He was unsuccessful. I left empty handed and I'm sorry to say I never did find out what had happened to her.

The D.C. riots were a shock to me. For the first time in my life I experienced American troops with drawn bayonets, threatening American citizens. It forced me to question my general philosophy. Naively, I had always believed that people were basically good and through my actions I could bring about social change. Now I realized that this rosy-eyed philosophy was out of touch with reality. I was no longer able to justify what I had believed in and had wanted to do. After much soul searching, I determined my social concerns about society were still important to me. I realized I had to continue doing what I had been doing all my life, slowly chipping away at the larger rock, even if my actions never did produce any major change.

The relevance of the District riots to my work on the Commission was dramatically underscored by the rioters' attacks on inner city merchants. For years many of these merchants had engaged in robbery by pen and were protected by the doctrine of caveat emptor (Let the buyer beware). Robbery by gun, however, was met by harsh criminal laws and often by brutal police practices. The difference between these two types of robbery was lost on the white establishment but not on the black community.

One aspect about the riots in D.C. that stood out in my mind was the line some of the rioters drew between the various businesses they attacked. Giant Foods, for example, had a good consumer reputation in the District. It was owned and operated by an old Washington family, the Danziger brothers. Esther Peterson was Giant's consumer representative and had been very active helping D.C. consumers find their way through the maze of supermarket aisles and products. The community trusted the company and posted several people outside the doors of a Giant Store in Northeast Washington to prevent it from being looted. When I was giving speeches to businesses around the country I often used that story to point out how important it was for them to be consumer minded because consumers were very much aware of a corporation's attitude towards them.

The FTC staff had always been reluctant to move against fly-by-night inner city scam artists who made a business of preying on the innocent.[1] Their concern was that these quick scam artists would move from place to place; if they were attacked for a practice, they would disappear, regroup and reincorporate under a different name and continue with their scams. The staff was also interested in getting the biggest bang for the Commission's buck. They focused on practices that were national in scope and tended to shy away from bringing cases against small retailers they believed were too local to affect nationwide practices.

My position was that the working poor normally patronized these small retailers, paid taxes and deserved protection. After much urging, the commissioners agreed with my argument and directed the staff to open a Metropolitan Fraud program in the District of Columbia.[1] As part of this program, the Commission prepared an economic report that showed there was a difference between what the lower and upper income wards paid for credit and products in the District.

When the report was about to be published, I experienced for the first time the power of the press. I heard that Bob Maynard of the *Washington Post* was writing a critical story on the FTC accusing us of holding back this report because of outside pressure. I called Maynard and invited him to my house to discuss his proposed article. When we met I told him how hard I had worked to get the report written and assured him that publication was only being delayed because of some last minute technical changes that had to be made. I pleaded with him to wait until the report was released before he published his article. He listened carefully, trying to determine if I was sincere. Finally, he agreed not to run the story and I promised to call him the instant the report was released. I was relieved. I knew there was nothing nefarious going on and I didn't want this important report tainted by vague suggestions of wrongdoing in its publication. This program not only impacted D.C. but the idea spread across the country. States began to enact laws modeled on the FTC program in the District that enabled them to move against their local scam artists.

Kent State followed the D.C. riots in May 1969. The image of the young woman weeping over the student shot by a National Guard trooper is burned forever in my mind. The night after the shooting I was scheduled to speak to a small cooperative in Greenbelt, Maryland. I could not bring myself to talk about the FTC, so I threw away my speech. I passionately talked about what had happened at Kent State, what I felt the country needed to do to stop this madness and how important it was to listen to those who disagreed with us. When I finished my speech, a member of the audience came up to me and pulled a pewter peace ring off her finger and pressed it into my hand. I cherish that ring to this day.

Of course, the Vietnam war was omnipresent. Students were increasingly vocal and mounting demonstrations in Washington, and I was deeply distressed over the way the Nixon administration treated the young protesters. The administration's response was to place them under arrest and then drag them on to rented city buses and carry them to some secret destination where they weren't able to contact lawyers or bring *habeas corpus* actions that would secure their freedom. They remained hidden for several days before they were finally located. All this in my country!

This was the political climate when I was invited to give the commencement address at American University. I decided to speak about the importance of young people expressing themselves and taking direct action on their beliefs. I also wanted to remind the graduates that the actions by the administration violated the free speech of the protesters. I wanted to share with them, by contrast, my own experiences on the Commission with some of the changes the Commission made in response to students' petitions.

I was very sensitive to the fact that I was a government official and that in one sense my speech could be viewed as a political act. So I talked with several people about the propriety of giving it. I remember showing the speech to Bob Pitofsky, the Director of the Commission's Bureau of Deceptive Practices. I respected his judgment. He was a balanced intellectual and also was someone who was familiar with the politics in Washington.

Bob was not upset about the propriety of my giving such a speech as a commissioner, but he was very upset at its focus. He, himself, was concerned about these Vietnam protesters interfering with government action, and feared that they might give the Nixon administration an excuse to crack down on any groups that opposed the government. He recalled that it was these types of highly emotional and angry antigovernment protesters that had given Hitler his excuse to crack down on the Jews in Germany and enact the anti Semitic laws.

At the same time, during a cocktail party at a friend's house, I had a similar argument with Judge Harold Green of the D.C. Superior Court. Judge Green shared a lot of Bob's fears about Nixon's reactions if the protesters continued their antiwar demonstrations. It was an interesting reaction. I didn't agree with these fears, and didn't feel they were reason enough for me to change my text or shy away from giving the speech. I gave it and it was well received.

I was happy and self-confident in my professional life at the FTC. I felt my time at the Commission was a wonderful validation of my years in analysis. I no longer felt I had a staff that hated me or resented working for me. As with all staff, of course, I am sure there were some who were dissatisfied but in the main we had a wonderful and productive time together. Sam Rozell, one of my attorney assistants, has sent me roses for my birthday every year since my term expired. Sam also periodically had called my FTC staff together to celebrate my various birthdays. We had fun reminiscing about our good times and they often mentioned how much that period meant to them. After all these years, we still see each other.

The last time I saw President Johnson was in 1972 when I was invited to give a speech on FTC advertising policy in Austin, Texas. Rand Dixon suggested I write LBJ and tell him I was coming. I did and when I arrived at the airport one of his aides met me and told me the president had laid out a luncheon at his library. Mary Grey, a prominent fundraiser for the Democratic Party, was also in attendance. Not only were the president's remarks enormously gracious, he also slipped into the first row of the auditorium where I was speaking. He must have been terribly lonesome for his role in government to sit though that! Then he wrote me a letter thanking me for coming to his library. This letter appears on the following page.

In 2002, the Commission honored me by naming their annual volunteerism award the Mary Gardiner Jones Award (Outstanding Volunteerism). The award recognizes an active employee whose volunteer efforts have benefited the community, the state, or the nation. The volunteer services may have been performed as an individual or as part of a group. The FTC chair, Tim Muris, announced the award:

> *[I] n honor of the FTC's first female commissioner and a tireless activist for the consumer cause who championed the Commission's role in protecting consumers. She sought to bolster the ranks of women lawyers and the FTC; she was the first commissioner to promote the use of consumer behavior research in Commission decisions and the first to hire a consumer research professional for her personal staff... Mary has for decades been an inspiration to anyone who would use their professional gifts as a community service volunteer.*

AUSTIN, TEXAS

Dear Mary:

I didn't think wild horses could bring me back from Acapulco, but, all it took were two very gracious, intelligent and charming Marys.

I enjoyed being with you and listening to your talk. It was a superb afternoon -- one I wouldn't have missed for the world. I hope you will come back one day and honor us with another visit.

With warm and grateful regards,

Sincerely,

Honorable Mary Gardiner Jones
Commissioner
Federal Trade Commission
Washington, D. C. 20580

February 28, 1972

My Commission years were the high point of my professional career. To be able to serve my government in this way, to wield a little power to make other peoples' lives a little better, and to have enough scope to use all of my talents and strengths was a rare privilege and one I will always treasure.

Notes

1. Much of the material that follows is drawn from my article entitled "The Federal Trade Commission in 1968: Times of Turmoil and Response," *Journal of Public Policy and Marketing,* vol. 7, pp.1-10 (1988).

Managing Editor and the first woman (second row, center) on the *Yale Law Journal* Board under the leadership of Louis Pollack (first row, center).

Again, the first woman at the law firm of Donovan Leisure Newton Lumbard and Irvine (William J. Donovan, second row to Mary's left).

General William J. Donovan (Wild Bill Donovan), head of the Wartime Intelligence Agency, the Office of Strategic Services and senior partner and founder of Donovan Leisure Newton Lumbard and Irvine. Mary worked for him in his law firm in New York City from 1948 to 1953.

Dr. Eugene A. Eisner, Mary's pyschoanalyst, and Mary.

Eugene and Margaret Eisner at their home in Scarsdale, N.Y.

Representative John L. Lindsay (R, N.Y.), who testified to Congress in support of Mary's appointment as commissioner to the Federal Trade Commission.

Reception at the White House for new Johnson appointees.

Mary in the Oval Office with President Lyndon B. Johnson learning about her appointment to the FTC as the first woman commissioner.

Sitting on the Federal Trade Commission.

Mary working with her administrative staff at the Federal Trade Commission.

Mary with her FTC professional staff at her 75th birthday celebration given by her staff.

Goodbye FTC, Hello Classroom

In 1973, when my term as Federal Trade Commissioner was due to expire, I began to think seriously about what I wanted to do next. I knew it would be inappropriate to put out feelers while I was still on the Commission; any law firm interested in me would probably have clients involved in antitrust or FTC issues. By the time my term ended, no law firm had approached me and I wasn't going to take the initiative to contact them.

I don't know if I made a conscious decision or not about seeking a law firm job, but, about this time, I was approached by Dave Gardner, a social marketer with the Commission, whose term at the Commission was coming to a close. Dave, who was planning to return to the University of Illinois, asked me if I would be interested in teaching there, and he specifically mentioned teaching at both the University's business and law schools. I said I was very interested indeed! Ever since high school, I had wanted to teach even though my one attempt at the George School was premature. Now I was ready; I had been through analysis, I had something to teach and the experience and maturity to back it up. So interviews were arranged, I flew out to Urbana and they went well. I was offered a joint appointment as a fully tenured professor in both schools and from that moment on I didn't give any other jobs a thought.

I was excited and immediately put my house up for sale and made arrangements to move to Illinois—a vague area of the country totally unknown to me. Not only had I never lived in the Midwest, I had never traveled in, through or around the farm belt. I should have been suspicious when every one I talked with at the university was eager to point out how easy it was to get away from Urbana; they stressed that there were direct flights to both Washington and New York. I didn't think anything about it at the time but I certainly understood after I got there.

Ann's only daughter, Abby, who was living with me at the time and my sister Betty, also living in Washington, offered to drive out with me to Urbana and help with the move. I was delighted. So, accompanied by my two cats and a car full of luggage, the three of us piled into my Mercedes sedan and set out for the "Heartland" together. We must have been quite a sight.

Abby had moved into my house in 1971, a year after she had graduated from Skidmore College. Originally, she had gone to Wisconsin with a boyfriend, but it didn't work out, and after a year of struggling to make ends meet, she called and asked if she could stay with me in Washington. I didn't know Abby very well as a child, but when she was twelve she visited me in Washington and two years later I invited her to join me in Paris where I was vacationing with my friend, Helen Nelson. We grew closer while she was in college. I would drive up to visit her because I had the feeling she was lonely and unhappy. So I was delighted when she wanted to come live with me in Washington and she proved to be a joy!

After a lot of effort on her part, Abby managed to land a much sought after internship with the Smithsonian Institution working on their summer Folk Life festival. She loved it, and by the end of the summer the Smithsonian, in a highly unusual move for them, hired her full time.

Unfortunately, after a year or so, her job got reclassified and she lost the health benefits she needed to pay for the psychoanalysis she had just started. I offered to help her financially, but she refused. With her usual determination and spunk, she quit the Smithsonian and found another job at the Government Printing Office which did pay benefits. She hated the job, but stuck it out and while there, applied for admission to George Washington University's School of Fine Arts.

She had asked her father for a loan to help with her tuition, but he refused and said he felt it would be more practical for her to move into business than seek a fine arts degree! It was a difficult time for Abby but she managed. Once again, even in the 1970s and the era of women's rights, women in my family still had to struggle for recognition and acceptance over what they wanted to do. I was proud of her.

I learned a lot about myself having Abby live with me. She was an independent soul who didn't feel a need to entertain me. She was comfortable with silence, and was perfectly happy reading or doing whatever she needed to do. It took me a while to adjust, but gradually I learned how to be myself with another person. I found I didn't have to entertain her, and I could go on with my own life even with another person in the house. It was lovely to share my thoughts and experiences with Abby and, in turn, enjoy what she was doing.

When I decided to go to Illinois, Abby was upset and said she wasn't quite ready to live on her own. But I knew I had to go. In typical fashion, she rolled with the punch, and in short order found a nice apartment on F Street, moved in, and did very well on her own.

When the three of us arrived in Urbana—luggage, cats and all—Betty and Abby helped me settle into the house I had rented from a law school professor who was away on sabbatical. Immediately after they left I began to search for a house to buy, and I found one close by on a beautiful tree lined street. It was an old-fashioned house, with a large front porch and a good-sized garden in the back. The owner of the house had loved gardening and left me a map of all the flowers—and weeds—that were in her garden. I loved that the house also had a large, dark paneled, unfinished attic with a high cathedral ceiling and immediately made plans to turn it into a music room. After a short search, I found a talented architect who had built a reputation for remodeling churches with high vaulted ceilings. I met with him a couple of times in the spring, told him what I wanted, and then went to Connecticut for the summer.

Margie Slocum Bearn, my law school classmate and former New York roommate, had bought a summer home in Stonington, Connecticut. I had told Margie that I wanted to retain a foothold in the east, now that I was about to launch my teaching career in the Midwest, and she enthusiastically recommended her area. During spring break in April 1974, I came east to look for a summer home, and found a charming old 1700s cottage with a walk-in fireplace, a birthing room and some of the original paneling. I purchased it immediately and moved in that summer.

When I returned to Urbana in the fall and walked into my house, I was stunned. The architect, Jack Baker, had created a spectacular room in the attic with stark white walls and a skylight, plus a large picture window that opened up the space to the outside world. But it was very different from the dark paneled room I had imagined. Plus, it had no wall space.

Jack had built shelves with indirect lighting in the short space between the sloped ceiling and the floor. It was certainly dramatic, but there were no corners for my very large stereo corner speakers. I no idea where I would put them. Jack, being helpful, said, "why don't you put them downstairs?" That wasn't my idea at all; this was to be my music room. Furthermore, I couldn't figure out where I would put my furniture. Again, he offered a suggestion: "Just buy bean bags or wicker furniture." That wasn't exactly my style either. But the room was beautiful.

By this time, Ann's third son, Charlie, was living with me. My version of why he came to Illinois is very different from his and each of us clearly remembers our own. Mine has Charlie saying, "Mary, if I can come out and live with you I'll go back to college." I had been urging him to do just that since he graduated from high school. Whatever the circumstances, Charlie came out in the fall of 1974, got himself admitted to Parkland Junior College, moved into my house and I was delighted. My relationship with him has always been special to me and the two of us go back a long way.

From the time Charlie was born, I had always thought of him as the coronation child. In June 1953, Ann was supposed to go to Queen Elizabeth's coronation but she was pregnant with Charlie who was due in July. Betty was living abroad at the time and she couldn't go either, so I was invited to go with Uncle Livy. We went first to Paris, and stayed in a lovely house on the Place de Vosges, whose previous owner, Marshall Singer, had known Sarah Bernhardt, the famous Parisian dancer. The story is that he would invite her to dance in his house as the musicians played on the little balcony overlooking the spacious living room.

After a week in Paris, we moved on to London for the coronation. We got up at 4 a.m., piled into our seats in Marlborough Park and watched all the hoopla during the daylong coronation parade. It was unbelievably exciting. By the time I got back to the states, Charlie had arrived.

Charlie was only six when his parents divorced, and during that traumatic time, he was shipped off to live with his nanny at her home in Tennessee. When he finally came back to Cold Spring Harbor, I can still see that small boy running around and poignantly asking, "Do you love me, do you love me?"

When Charlie was twelve, he was visiting me in Washington when the walk on the moon took place. He was very excited and wanted to tape the walk so he rushed downstairs to my den to look for some audiotapes. The only ones he could find contained some of my speeches that were "sacrificed" in favor of the space walk; we agreed it was a better use of my cassettes!

Attending community college was a difficult transition for Charlie and he was sensitive about it. If I would ask him about his college work in what I thought was an innocuous way, he would bristle and think I was telling him what to do. I didn't realize it at the time, but that is probably exactly what I was doing because I was so up tight about my own teaching. We gingerly tiptoed around each other but I tried very hard to make sure he had enough space to do whatever he needed to do.

Fortunately, we both loved the old house. Charlie is very talented and knew immediately what needed to be done to make the renovated attic into a workable music room. He built "corners" for the speakers that acted as buffers. We did buy those beanbags Jack had suggested and I'm still devoted to them. The new attic became our favorite room and proved to be an ideal setting for the seminars I held for my students.

I learned to appreciate our wonderful old-fashioned front porch. When I would leave in the morning or come home in the evening, my neighbors would wave and greet me. I learned to wave back! Porches are a great social institution and I appreciate why so many of the houses used to have them; they add to a sense of community. Also, I went everywhere on my bicycle, including the local bank where everyone addressed me by my first name. I hated this when I lived in Washington but for some reason, in Urbana, I accepted it as their way of being friendly. I managed to make good friends in both faculties, but I observed that, as a rule, faculty members were loners; their lives were either in the classroom, in the library, or at home with their families.

I had been strongly influenced by my experience at Yale Law School and was curious about how the Illinois School of Law viewed its students. I wondered if they had a specific philosophy that guided their teaching. They didn't, nor did they have a particular vision of what an ideal lawyer should be. Furthermore, they didn't apparently feel it was necessary to have one. I realized I was naïve, and probably wrong in assuming that a vision would be an important part of any law school education.

My experience as a tenured professor was not as exciting as I had hoped. At the beginning of each semester, I found it difficult to prepare course outlines and appropriate reading materials because I didn't know the literature and had never done that kind of research. Plus, I felt uncomfortable standing before the class as an authority figure. I didn't want to just lecture; I wanted the students to discuss what they were reading. Students love to talk but I was not skilled enough to get them to integrate their reading assignments into their discussions. This was particularly true for my business school students. I needed to develop a focus that could guide both my class preparation and my teaching.

The business school students would end up talking about business problems they'd heard about or they knew from their own experience; all without benefit from any of the readings. One of my goals was to make the business students aware of the issues that affected consumers and I wanted them to handle policy issues more systematically. My inexperience showed and only after much trial and error, did my business school policy discussions improve.

I remember one discussion we had about the pros and cons of creating a federal Consumer Protection Agency. Several students I had tagged as conservatives spoke in favor of such an agency, while others who opposed it did so with rational arguments. I was pleased.

At my invitation, the father of one of my students, a corporate chief executive officer, addressed the class while he was in town. I suggested the class prepare some questions for him. They looked perfectly blank. But when the time arrived and I called on them, generally I found most of their questions were perceptive. I also learned to call on some of the students who never volunteered in class and when I did, I found they were doing some good thinking. My big lesson was learning how not to confuse inarticulate or shy students as being bored or disinterested. Some of the quietest students in class turned out to be interested, warm and outgoing outside the classroom.

My law school classes reflected some of my same inexperience; I would get a good class discussion going, only to interject something into the discussion and the focus would turn on me. This made the discussion disintegrate and for me, it was a constant live and learn situation.

In general, my law school classes were better than those in the business school because I was able to organize them more coherently; they made more sense. Also, the students were better prepared and more accustomed to talking in class. Still, I was dissatisfied and the fact that my expertise was in law rather than in business was no consolation. After some sound advice from a law school colleague, I realized that one of the things missing in my teaching was a focus on what practitioners needed to know, as well as what issues they should be aware of as citizens. This helped in my classroom preparation, but it didn't relieve my anxieties and self-doubt.

I faced some fascinating dilemmas in the law school. One of my students wrote a stunning brief on a topic I had assigned; well written in a breezy, easy flowing manner, but I couldn't imagine how a judge would react to this type of "non-lawyerlike" writing. My dilemma became how to grade him? Would I be doing him a disservice by giving him a high grade or would I frustrate his creativity by marking him down because he chose to be unconventional? I compromised by talking with him. But, in the end, I was confined by what I presumed were the standards of law schools and the law profession.

The conservatism of the law students also surprised me. When we talked about marketplace deceptions, I found the law students were willing to accept almost any business practice designed to lure consumers into buying their products, and accepted as reasonable the argument that business didn't have to pay attention to the ethics of their practices. They were willing to accept the marketplace as a jungle and "caveat emptor" as its guiding principle. I tried unsuccessfully to get them to question this belief, and I found their complacency frustrating.

The law students' lack of concern was in surprising contrast to many of my business school students who sparkled in these discussions and were deeply concerned about ethical issues. Yet others of the business school students seemed indifferent; they looked bored and asked what we were doing and why. I sensed many of the students were eager for direct teacher contact and they would come into my office just to talk. One told me he joined my class because he liked the reading list; another came to my office excited about a book he had heard reviewed on the radio concerning consumer complaints. He brought me the tape of the broadcast and asked if he could do his assigned book review on that topic. He also said most of his classes ended with the bell, but my classes were so stimulating that the students continued talking over lunch about issues that had been raised in class. I began to hold my seminar on social responsibility in the attic of my house and the students appeared to like that; some came and stayed all day.

Gradually, I began to see some success, but emotionally I wasn't satisfied. I found it took all the will power I could muster to prepare for classes. My energy was scattered and I had difficulty digging into one specific issue. I would think about writing an article, would start it and then get diverted. I dabbled at preparing the next year's course but found it difficult to focus. Some of my emotional demons were still at play and contributing to my feelings of insecurity. Fortunately, by now I could recognize what was going on inside of me, and I could deal with it positively rather than immediately assume that I was totally incapable of teaching.

I began to realize that a lot of what I was going through was decompressing from the headiness of my term at the FTC, while, at the same time, I was trying to learn a new craft. I always found myself more comfortable when I was away from the campus and giving speeches about the consumer movement or the regulatory process. So I tried to dig in and learn my craft.

While I was at Illinois, I was named a trustee of Colgate University. They had just gone coed, while Wellesley, where I was also a trustee, had just decided against it. In my role as trustee at both colleges, I focused my energies on the students.

At Wellesley, I worked closely with faculty and students who were deeply involved in supporting South African blacks fighting against that country's obscene apartheid policy. I also chaired the trustee's Subcommittee on Social Responsibility, composed of students and faculty, as well as trustees.

Leon Sullivan, a black minister in Philadelphia, who was also an entrepreneur and a member of the Board of Directors of General Motors, had drawn up a set of investment and employment principles for American corporations to follow in South Africa. Conforming to the "Sullivan Principles" became a rallying cry for the pro-divestiture groups forming on many American college campuses.

The students at Wellesley, however, wanted their Board of Trustees to go further: They wanted the board to divest itself of stock in any company that had holdings in South Africa, regardless of whether or not the company conformed to the Sullivan Principles.

As a subcommittee, we tried to get the board to go along with the students and on one occasion almost succeeded, but lost by one vote. The board then got savvy about our lobbying and we never got that close again. They were adamant in their refusal to divest themselves of stocks in companies that simply maintained a business presence in South Africa. However, they did agree that in the future they would no longer invest in any company that refused to sign the Sullivan Principles. We had made some progress.

I found the advocacy by the Wellesley students impressive. When we held a trustees meeting on campus, the students held a candlelight vigil outside the College Club, where the trustees stayed. They also mounted mime portrayals on the steps of the library where we met showing the effects of apartheid on the blacks. Student opposition was essentially non violent, and only once did it erupt into a more active protest. The students occupied the Administration building where the president, Nan Kohane, had her office. She took them food, but eventually had to call the police to force them out.

I was less active on the Colgate board—the lone woman on a board of very conservative Colgate alumni. I saw my role as lending support to the faculty in their efforts to make coeducation work on this formerly male-dominated campus. I also tried to support the students in their requests to have a student representative on the Board of Trustees. However, when the board decided the students weren't serious about the issue because their requests were so polite, I exploded: "Do you really want students to burn down a building before you take them seriously?

Yet, on another occasion, the board totally surprised me. They took a very strong position against the Colgate president for not acting decisively against some Delta Kappa Epsilon fraternity students who participated in the gang rape of a fellow student. The board, instead of acting like fraternity brothers and saying, "boys will be boys," suddenly became outraged fathers of daughters and almost fired the president for not taking strong enough disciplinary steps against both the students involved and the fraternity.

These other student concerns were very much on my mind when I was at Illinois. As my classes progressed, I began to think my contribution, as a professor, would be mostly in the area of student-teacher relationships. I had always enjoyed being around young people and found it easy to relate to them. Yet I also knew I owed them a good, substantive course that would stimulate their critical thinking. While it satisfied me emotionally to help them reflect on who they were, and what they wanted to be, it didn't justify my tenure as an academic professor. Also, I wasn't prepared to do the research and writing so important in academia. I recognize its importance and applaud it; it helps you stay fresh and excited about new ideas. But I wasn't prepared to do that kind of research or to spend the necessary long hours in the library. Above all, I was terrified that after twenty years I would be in a rut and still talking about "When I was a Federal Trade Commissioner.... " I had waited too long to enter the academic world and I missed the action and decision-making I was used to. University teaching was not for me. It was time to leave.

When I told Ken Uhl, the Dean of the Business School, about my decision to leave, he understood completely. He said it was hard for policy makers with all their experience in the "real world," to join the rarified atmosphere of the academic world. Then he added, it was particularly hard for easterners to come to the Midwest. I demurred over all of it, "Your world is just as real as mine. It's just different and less action-oriented." I'm not sure I convinced him, but I do believe it.

As for the Midwest, I believe most of us stay attached to the geographic environment we grew up in. I was ready to go home and so was Charlie. Both of us had the same reaction to the farm belt; we were overwhelmed by the sameness. Beyond the carefully platted farmlands you can see the horizon for miles and miles and there are relatively few curves in the road. Everything is flat. It made me realize how emotionally attached I was to the hills and the dips and curves in the narrow roads where I had grown up. Charlie would ask, "When are we going home, Mary?" and I would answer, "as soon as I can find another job, Charlie."

I did some job searching at law firms, and had some interesting discussions with a Chicago firm that was looking for a lawyer to head up their new antitrust section in their Washington office. I realized it would be perfect for me, but I was apprehensive about my abilities. I had trouble imagining myself running an antitrust office, which, I realize now was ridiculous, but I think my apprehension showed. Eventually, our discussions petered out, but the hesitation was more on my part than on theirs.

Then *mirabile dictu,* a consumer friend of mine, Helen Nelson, who had been Consumer Advisor to California's Governor Pat Brown, called and told me about a job. Helen had been approached by Western Union to help them set up and head a new Department of Consumer Affairs but had turned it down. Helen then referred them to me. Western Union was looking for someone at the executive vice president level and it sounded good to me. I called them, and we arranged to meet in Chicago. The first interview went well, and I had a second at their corporate headquarters in Upper Saddle River, New Jersey. I met with Earl Hilburn, the chairman of the board and was hired.

I returned to Illinois, said my goodbyes, sold my house, and eagerly packed up. After a year and a half, Charlie and I left the Midwest and headed home.

Coming Home to Washington and Exploring the Corporate World

I had spent spring break looking for a house in Washington so when my last semester of teaching was over, Charlie and I were ready to move right in. I loved the house. It was a little more spacious than my West Lane Keys house, the first home I purchased in Washington. Better yet, it needed little work to be done on it. I have always preferred "instant houses," as remodeling never appealed to me. Charlie had successfully transferred his Parkland College credits to George Washington University so that he could finish his college education. But our relationship in Washington was different.

While we lived in Illinois we were relatively dependent on each other, but we both had friends in Washington and felt freer to come and go. As a result, I was never sure if and when Charlie would be home for dinner or expected dinner. I found myself trying to pin Charlie down as to his plans so I could make mine, prepare meals and shop. So, I solved the eating dilemma by buying a microwave oven! I would keep things frozen and would unfreeze them if he turned up unexpectedly.

With the exception of Charlie rather than Abby living with me, my life was pretty much the same as it had been while I was at the Federal Trade Commission. Betty's husband was retired and they were still living in Washington. Abby was comfortably settled in her own apartment and back working at the Smithsonian in a job that paid benefits, and John, Charlie's oldest brother, was now working as a psychiatric social worker and living in Washington. I loved the idea of being back in Washington close to my family. Of course, we all had our own lives but we saw each other fairly frequently, and with my analysis behind me I was more able to reach out to them.

When I joined Western Union in 1975, the company was going through an important shift in direction; moving away from what it had always been—a 125-year-old regulated communications company—and attempting to transform itself into a more competitive enterprise. Also, deregulation was breathing down its neck and it was getting competition from the new telecommunications technologies that were transmitting information by satellite, telephone and cable. Western Union did have West Star, the first commercial satellite, but this advanced technology was expensive to operate and traffic was slow to develop. Furthermore, the company had a major investment in its telex network and too little available cash to successfully write it off. This was in direct contrast to IBM, the communication behemoth that had enough cash reserves in the late 1950s to eliminate its punch card machines, enabling them to move aggressively into the new era of computers and wireless communications. Unfortunately, its lack of ready cash forced Western Union to stick with its telex network while the rest of the world was gearing up for the new electronic computers rapidly emerging in the marketplace.

This was the atmosphere when I was hired as Vice President for Consumer Affairs, an office newly created to bring the company into closer contact with its customers. I was apprehensive about entering these corporate halls, afraid I might lose my sensitivity to consumer issues and concerned about the reception I'd get internally as a former regulator and consumer advocate. But I was encouraged and pleased by Earl Hilborn's support. As Chairman of the Board, he issued a press release to the general media that was also carried in the company's newspaper:

> *We are extremely fortunate to have Miss [Mary Gardiner] Jones join our executive Staff. With her breadth of experience and nationally recognized in both academic and pubic life, we will be well advised and directed in consumer affairs.*

My fellow executives were polite but a little concerned about this "consumer" person who was a lawyer and a former regulator coming on board without any real experience in the corporate world. But following Earl's leadership, they gave me the benefit of the doubt and slowly I wove my way into their corporate culture. I'm not sure I would have lasted in a truly cutthroat competitive environment. Western Union was a family-oriented company; it was not unusual to find husbands and wives, fathers and sons, mothers and daughters—entire families—working for the company. It was a company whose employees loved the company and had been there through several generations.

But there was one exception to this rosy scenario that reminded me of my past job-hunts at the various New York law firms. This time, however, it happened after I was hired and I was much more able to deal with it, thanks to my analysis.

As the new executive, my first step was to make an appointment to see the company General Counsel who ran the Washington office. I made the appointment, we met and he politely showed me around. Then he pointed to a small office next to his and said I could use this and "please, feel free to use his secretary any time." I knew immediately that would never work, so I suggested we look at other office space. I had spotted two vacant offices down the hall with additional space for a secretary and told him I thought we could break down the wall between the two offices and make one large room big enough to hold my books and files. Then I made clear I needed my own secretary and she could sit comfortably in the space outside the two offices. I added I was sure I would have too many demands on his secretary to make sharing a secretary feasible. He was furious and said he would have to check with company headquarters in Upper Saddle River.

The next day I got a call from Earl Hilborn suggesting I come to Upper Saddle River and talk over my new responsibilities. When I arrived I learned that I was to have two offices; one in Washington and one in Upper Saddle River. The first thing he did was show me an enormous office and then nervously asked if it was big enough. I was embarrassed, but decided to go along and agreed that indeed the space would be fine. That ended the discussions about office space; when I got back to Washington, work had already started on combining the two offices I had wanted.

I was rather proud of myself. This was the first time in my professional life I had aggressively spoken up on my own behalf; without realizing it, I had become a more confident professional. Analysis had given me self-confidence and I found I could be politically savvy about my role as Western Union's first female executive.

This was my introduction to the corporate world, but getting used to it took more time. Once I sent Earl Hilburn a memorandum about a particular issue I thought he should be aware of. Someone in Earl's office got a good laugh at this and told me they were sure it was the first memorandum Earl had ever received with footnotes!

Also, I learned corporations don't have problems—they have challenges! I found this shift in language helpful—somehow having a challenge is more affirmative than having to deal with a problem. I wish I would have had my corporate experience before I was named to the Federal Trade Commission. The management tools I learned at Western Union would have been helpful to me as a commissioner as I worked with both my own staff and Commission staff. I could have been a more productive manager in addition to my policy and judicial responsibilities, and perhaps learned how to focus on giving fewer instructions to the staff, placing more emphasis on the outcomes we desired and letting staff reach these goals in their own way.

Stepping into the corporate environment, my biggest concern was that once I was behind the corporate walls, I would lose my sensitivity to consumer issues. Fortunately I found they were deeply ingrained in me even though I had to learn to adapt them to the corporate world.

As a regulated company, Western Union's business was divided between its telex and satellite services to commercial clients and its telegraph and money order business that focused on individual consumers. Both parts of its business were subject to the rules of the Federal Communications Commission that declared all customers must be treated on a first come, first served basis.

This meant if the telex machine of the Chairman of the Chase Manhattan Bank or of the Israeli Defense Ministry malfunctioned, their company went into the same waiting line as the smallest mom and pop operation. In a strange role reversal, I found myself trying to persuade the telex repair people to treat the Director of the Israeli New York Defense Office or the Chairman of the Board of Chase Manhattan, with special consideration. Fairness among customers was very important to me, but some of the company's practices had to bend a little because Western Union was confronted with intense competition from the new telecommunications technologies. I found myself focusing most of my energies on helping Western Union deal with their business customers.

I asked for advice from George Brown, a friend who had been Marketing Director of the Ford Motor Company and later was the Director of the United States Census Bureau. At the time, George was at the census bureau but was generous with his advice and help. He suggested I develop a satisfaction survey among Western Union's corporate customers to measure the performance of Western Union's service staff and help management look at its own performance. This, he said, would provide me with a useful performance benchmark for the company.

Initially, the company's staff resisted, but gradually they began to understand the importance of learning how a customer viewed their service. If our customers thought of our service or repair personnel as always late, even if our staff's records showed they had responded in a reasonable time, then something was wrong with their customer communications. The telex survey turned out to be a valuable tool for the company and gradually enhanced my image within the company.

Western Union's telegram, mailgram and money order business was the weakest link in Western Union's performance and directly affected their public image. As I gained the trust of the various employees in the Western Union field offices who dealt with this part of the business, I would receive telephone calls from the company's field managers who were stationed all over the country. They managed Western Union's telegram, mailgram and money order business and called me about the Western Union sales practices they disapproved of, requesting that I discuss their complaints with the president.

Several times field staff complained to me that Western Union's money order business was priced too high and that lower income customers, who depended on this service, couldn't afford the higher prices Western Union was charging. I began to play an internal role as intermediary between our field and marketing staffs that eventually improved service to all our customers. I took the pricing issue up with the president who told me he was very aware of many of the issues being raised by field staff but the company had no other option if it was to stay in business. In a nutshell, I found this was the difference between public service and the corporate world; government public servants are paid to resolve problems for the benefit of the public whereas the mission of the corporate world is to make profits for its shareholders.

Western Union had a regulatory obligation to serve all telegraph customers equally regardless of the content of the message with one exception, if the telegram contained obscene words it must be rejected. In the 1960s and 70s, American culture was rapidly changing; language once thought to be objectionable had become part of the common jargon. Western Union telegraph operators had trouble catching up. My role was to teach the operators that words we once considered obscene were no longer objectionable—a strange role for this lady executive!

Within the corporation, the old politeness rules still applied: When I came into meetings, everyone jumped to their feet, or if someone used the word "damn," all heads would turn in my direction to make sure I wasn't fainting away. Little did they know what I was telling their field operators!

Later, as some of the executives got to know me, they came to me and asked if I would please restrain their newly hired women from asserting their independence and giving the men a hard time about how they were being treated. I answered, "No way." I might still be a member of the "politeness cult" but I didn't like being there. I told them quite frankly I was glad their women employees were speaking up for themselves and making it clear they were equal and entitled to respect.

The one thing I never understood about the corporate world was its lack of intellectual conversation. I had seen this on the various corporate boards I sat on and once again I was confronting it at Western Union. With the exception of the president, none of my fellow Western Union executives ever talked about a play they'd seen, a book they'd read or music they had liked. The only social thing they seemed comfortable talking about was sports. Or they would tell jokes. Perhaps that has changed, but it was glaringly apparent in my day in the corporate culture. One of the executives dealt with this by not going to the hospitality suite after the meetings were over. I always went. I was afraid to stand out and afraid of being different. I think I just wanted to be regarded as one of them, one of the "boys."

Now, in my fourth career, I was working in a 125-year-old regulated company trying to help them become more competitive. I found myself far removed from my passion—and power—to make the consumer movement part of the basic decision-making process in our company beyond what I could do as one person. Fortunately, despite the policy limitations of the job, I found the challenges intellectually stimulating although not emotionally rewarding and I learned a lot. Plus, I had a wonderful staff.

Western Union was a federal contractor and was required by law to have employees that reflected the total population of the area where they were located. I wanted to go a step further, however, and was determined to hire as many minorities as possible. I made a concerted effort to recruit staff from as broad a background as possible and made certain that any announcement of staff vacancies would appear in the minority press as well as the traditional outlets.

My first employee was my secretary, Janice Miller, a stunning African-American woman who appeared for our first interview looking very chic and sophisticated in a simple black dress with a white collar. I hired her on the spot. We worked well together for the entire time I was with Western Union and we continue to remain in touch. As the years have gone by it's been a thrill to see Janice move into management.

However, some of my other efforts at hiring minority staff were less successful. I have never been good at evaluating people; if they have a sunny smile I like them and assume they are capable. My staff finally came to me and suggested I let them do the initial screening of candidates. I had to agree. We had fewer problems after they took over and we still managed to keep our record of hiring minority staff at all levels in my office.

A lot of my work involved customer complaints. Before I came, Bill Killian had handled this work in the office. Bill, a southerner from Winston-Salem, North Carolina whose wife also worked with the company, was devoted to the company's consumers but his style was very different from mine and I hesitated to make him a part of my staff. I wasn't sure I could relate to someone so very different, so very "Southern."

Fortunately, I decided to ask Bill to join my staff and it was a lucky move on my part. His skills were invaluable and he had great loyalty to me and enormous dedication to our customers. When he died from a sudden heart attack, my staff and I went to North Carolina for his funeral. Winston-Salem was an unfamiliar culture to me and I went down with all my pre- conceived notions about the insincerity of southern politeness. I found out how wrong I was. At Bill's funeral the warmth and charm of his family and friends enveloped us and for the first time in my life I learned what southern hospitality was all about. They extended themselves to make sure we felt welcome!

Customer complaints were an early warning sign of Western Union's consumer problems. We developed a way to manage the data we received and then we fed it back to the staff so they could see how their corporate clients and customers perceived them.

One of Western Union's major difficulties was their practice of having the billing department take responsibility for handling consumer complaints; billing clerks, accustomed to dealing only with "dead beats," were not trained how to listen to consumers. Instead, they were rude and indifferent. Unfortunately, our efforts to train the billing staff to have greater sensitivity to consumer complaints were not realistic and we also failed to get this responsibility shifted to another section of the company. Another "challenge" I faced was to include the quality of customer service in the annual review of a manager's performance. I strongly believed that until customer service was measured it would never receive the same priority as selling the product. This took a lot of pushing and I am not sure I was ever successful.

Working at Western Union, I had more free time for a social life than when I lived in Washington as a Federal Trade Commissioner. As I pursued my new corporate career I faced a different personal dilemma; I began to date a widower who was an old friend of mine from my FTC days. We saw a lot of each other, became very close, and traveled together to Greece. He was eager to get married but I was hesitant and said I needed more time. Wiser than I, he told me he wondered if I ever would be ready. I had to admit that was probably true and we decided to separate. Eventually he married again and fortunately, we have remained good friends.

This was also the time I took on the presidency of the National Consumer's League, the oldest consumer organization in the country. Esther Peterson had been the first president and Caroline Ware, a long time consumer activist, was on the board. Unfortunately, and true to form, I had difficulty sharing authority with the paid executive director, who I felt didn't have a strong commitment to the consumer movement, and I pushed to take over certain key areas of her responsibility. I wasn't able to successfully wage a power struggle and I certainly wasn't adept at playing the political game. I knew I had the board's respect but I failed to seek their support. After talking it over with the board chair, a friend of mine, I realized I couldn't win that struggle and it would be better for everyone if I resigned. Once again I was left to wonder if this wasn't just another example of my difficulty in sharing authority.

New problems were beginning to surface in my personal life; my career was going well but I was depressed, lonely and unable to express myself. As I broadened my social life, I found myself overly concerned with other people's reaction to me and afraid of losing their friendship. It began to get dysfunctional so I decided to go back into therapy. I wanted to gain some insight into my feelings of inadequacy and try to understand why I had these debilitating feelings despite a "successful" career. I yearned for inner security and longed to be at peace with myself.

I decided to try group therapy. Many of my problems involved relationships and I thought being in a group would give me an opportunity to explore my feelings with others. I became deeply involved with members of the group and when I did talk, I found myself reciting a litany of what I most hated about myself. Also I felt I was being ignored by our group therapist, Bill Kraus. At the same time, I would worry that what I had said was boring or I was talking about inconsequential things or I was taking time from the other members of the group. It wasn't successful. After about a year, I came to the conclusion I couldn't handle group therapy because I was too self-absorbed and wasn't able to benefit from the input of my fellow group members. I decided I needed one-on-one therapy.

I was referred to a psychoanalyst, Dr. Henry Siegel, who was very different from Gene Eisner. I saw him only three days a week instead of the five when I was in analysis with Gene. Henry was more participatory and tried to help me out of my silent moods. Also, for the first time, I explored my early childhood, my ambiguous relationships with men, my dating and the continuing difficulties I experienced interacting with others—male or female. Henry pointed out all human beings seek unconditional love but primarily in their infancy; I was still looking for that kind of love. It took many months for me to realize this, of course, but when I did, it made a huge difference in my life. It seems clear to me now that what I went through with Gene was an exploration of my adolescence and with Henry my early childhood.

Tragically, during this time, my wonderful niece, Abby, was killed in an automobile accident. Her death was a devastating blow for the entire family and for me it was like losing my daughter.

It was September 1980, just three months after she had married Doug Bernon whom she had met the previous Halloween at a party in Washington. Jokingly, she said she couldn't remember his name so she referred to him as the Pumpkin Man. Abby was back working at the Smithsonian at the time and was coming back from one of the museum warehouses when she was sideswiped by a D.C. garbage truck and thrown from the car. Immediately she was taken by helicopter to the Washington Hospital Center where they struggled to save her life.

Charlie got the word and immediately called me. He and his friend, later his wife, Lynne Highberg, were both working in the Ecological Services Laboratory of the National Park Service. They rushed home and we met at my house and went together to the hospital where Abby lingered for several days before she died. Her mother, Ann, her father, her brothers and Betty were already there.

The hospital made a room available to us, and numb from shock, we sat together and just waited. One of Abby's friends sat with her in the intensive care unit but I couldn't bring myself to go in there to see her hooked up to the tubes and wires they tether patients to in an effort to save their lives.

I haven't ever gotten over Abby's death. I am not sure anyone ever gets over the loss of a beloved family member or close friend. After a while the acute pain diminishes but it remains just below the surface. An unexpected event—almost anything—causes the emotional pain to erupt and manifest itself all over again. Her death has left an indelible scar.

That first evening after her death several of my friends came over to the house, including my analyst Henry Segal; that moved me very much and it was comforting to be with them. But what really got me through that terrible time was "sitting shiva" at Doug and Abby's house. Doug, who was brought up in a Jewish household, held that wonderful ritual for three days with their friends coming and staying most of the day. I felt surrounded by the enormous love we all shared for Abby and Doug. We buried Abby in our family cemetery in Cold Spring Harbor. My nephew David had given Doug an airline ticket to Europe so he could get away and grieve. And after the funeral Ann and the rest of the family went their separate ways.

The Smithsonian's annual Folk Life Festival, on which Abby had been working so hard before the accident, ended the week after she died. Ralph Rinzler, the director of the festival, dedicated the closing session of the summer festival to her. At the time of the dedication, I was the only family member present. Several of the Native American and Vietnamese groups who had exhibited on the Mall were there and made very touching remarks about Abby. The dedication ceremony was at the same time, both heartbreaking and heartwarming.

Through the years, Doug and I have remained close. I talked to Henry a lot about Abby's death and my love for Doug and wondered if I should stop seeing Doug because it might be too painful for him. Henry said, "Let Doug decide that." He was right.

The next year, Doug went to San Diego to work on a Ph.D. in clinical psychology. Whenever I went out to Los Angeles I would visit him and it was wonderful to have someone to cry with. Doug received his degree and returned to Washington to practice.

Ten years later he met and married a sweet and accomplished woman, Bernadette Brennan, who was the editor of *Sailing World*, a large magazine owned by the *New York Times*. Bernadette and Doug had met through their shared love of sailing. The wedding took place in Newport, Rhode Island where Bernadette lived, and was attended by all of Doug and Abby's friends. It was a bittersweet experience, but Bernadette is a lovely person and I am so happy that she and Doug found each other.

Abby's youngest brother, Rob, was particularly devastated by her death. Rob was the only child of Ann's second marriage to Bob Crooker and he grew up with Bob's three sons who were in and out of the house at that time, as well as Ann's youngest children, David, Abby and Charlie. Rob's parents were considerably older than his classmates' parents. A moody child, Rob looked to Abby as his refuge from this large extended family.

Rob grew up playing the role of mediator between the Crooker and Watkins children who were living at home from time to time when he was growing up. I think Rob has always been closer to his Watkins half brothers and to Bill Crooker, the youngest Crooker child who had lived for a much longer period in the family home than the older Crooker brothers who had grown up mostly in Chicago before their father's marriage to my sister.

Rob, a gifted and kind young man, graduated from Princeton School of Engineering and later took an MBA at the Massachusetts Institute of Technology. My mother had named me trustee of Rob's share of some money she left her grandchildren at her death (not trusting the ability of Ann and her husband, Bob to handle money). This made for a good deal of friction between Rob, his father and me over my handling of his money. I got quite huffed but Abby and Charlie intervened to simmer me down. They reminded me that Rob was just a youngster at the time and, of course, close to his father, who was probably rightfully miffed at mother's slight to him and Ann. I was happy Abby and Charlie intervened, as I treasure my relationship with Rob and wouldn't have wanted anything to mar it.

Rob writes lovely poetry and is a fine photographer. Early in his career, he quit his engineering job on Long Island and went to Germany for a year to immerse himself in the language and write poetry. He was dating a German girl at the time, Susanne, whom he eventually married. The entire Watkins and Jones families, and Bill Crooker, attended the wedding in Heidelberg—a happy occasion—and I tried to resurrect my rusty German.

Rob and Susanne came back to the States and settled in Cambridge. Rob was at Arthur D. Little and Susanne at Tufts University in the German department. But she was homesick, and for a variety of reasons they decided to return to Germany to live. Rob, with his excellent German, got a job with an old line German printing firm responsible for transitioning the company into the modern printing and communications technologies. His mediating skills as a young child have undoubtedly been enormously helpful to him in bridging the old and the new technologies and the German and American cultures and he has done exceedingly well. They now have an adorable daughter, Hannah, who is obviously the apple of her father's eye. Fortunately she is growing up bilingual, something that will stand her in good stead throughout her life. Susanne left her English translation job to have more time with Hannah and takes her daughter to swimming classes, pre-kindergarten and now kindergarten. She is also teaching English to a small group of children weekly.

I have remained close to all of Ann's children. John, her oldest son, was the first of her children to land on my doorstep. One evening, when I was living in New York, John showed up; his wife Bonnie had left him and together with their four-year-old son, John Townsend, had gone home to her parents in Ohio. I had never met young JT, as they called him, who had been born in Nigeria when John had gone there after Yale to teach English. John was devastated over the separation and wanted to go into analysis. It was then he told me he was homosexual. Bonnie also called me several times wanting to know whether she had done the right thing. I was, of course, deeply concerned but I had no advice to give to either of them.

My mother's reaction was the opposite. She insisted they must stay married at all costs and divorce was unnecessary. All John had to do—and she would help—was set himself up in his own apartment so he could lead his own life. Her model, of course, was her homosexual brother, Livy, and my mother accepted her role as his hostess and cover. John, however, was clear that under no circumstances would he live a life of such duplicity.

John moved to Washington where he worked at the DC Department of Human Rights and later at the Washington Urban League. He was always close to Betty and they shared deep religious convictions that Betty expressed all her life in her volunteer service in the church. She was one of the first church leaders to work to open relations between the black and white congregations in the District.

Although Betty, John and I all shared our concerns for building closer and more respectful relationships with Washington's African-American community, I was never able to share their devotion to the church. John really immersed himself in the life of the African-American community and made most of his friends among the blacks. I think he often grew impatient with me—and perhaps with Betty—because we did not immerse ourselves as much as he did in that community. After he got his social work degree at Howard and Catholic universities he worked as a therapist almost exclusively with black patients.

I continued to be close to my extended family and because my work at Western Union allowed me more free time, I was able to take advantage of the opportunities opening up for women, and accepted various offers of appointments on national corporate boards, once again providing me with some interesting new experiences.

Corporate Boards, a Woman's Advantage

For the first time in my life, being a professional woman with consumer expertise began to be an advantage. The first board I was asked to join was the Safeway Corporation Board of Directors in Oakland, California. The consumer movement was in its ascendancy and women associated with that movement were very attractive candidates for a high intensity consumer retailer like Safeway.

While serving on the board, I was able to push hard for the advancement of Safeway's female employees, who held few of the managerial jobs. Women were mainly employed in the lower ranks as bag "boys" or checkout clerks. Their route to the top was non-existent. Safeway maintained they had tried hard to find women for upper management jobs but they were unsuccessful in their search. I began to look into their promotion practices and found the problem was their preconceived notion of what type of manager would be successful based solely on their experience with male managers. I tried to point out that women have their own style and didn't necessarily fit into the male model. But it was difficult to reach those who did the hiring. Unfortunately, a majority of the directors didn't feel as strongly about the issue as I did, and during my tenure on the board I was not able to make it a company priority. They were unfailingly polite but made it clear that the issue was not one of high corporate importance.

I also concerned myself with the timing of a salary increase they intended to give their chief executive, Bill Mitchell. These were the Carter years (1976) when the country was struggling with runaway inflation and President Carter was urging both labor and management to hold down their wage and price demands. Another board member agreed with me about the timing of the salary increase, but the rest of the board disagreed: "You don't understand, Mary, Bill Mitchell's salary is fifteenth among the salaries of members in San Francisco's Economic Club" (an elite group of businessmen in the Bay area). As I recall, that consideration was more important than either President Carter's concerns with inflation or the CEO's performance; neither of which was even discussed.

Another question I had raised during my tenure on the board was whether Safeway, as a major consumer of electricity, was doing enough to push the electric companies in San Francisco to keep down the price of electricity. My question evoked a passionate response from one of the board members, who called attention to the high costs the electric energy industry was experiencing.

When I looked at my board list, I realized the man who was speaking was the Chairman of the Board of Pacific Gas and Electric, the largest electric company on the west coast. After the meeting, he drove me back to San Francisco and we had a chance to talk. I said he must find it difficult to balance the company's needs for profits against his customers' needs for low cost energy. I thought it was unfair that they should have to choose between electricity, or food or doctor's bills. Looking out over the San Francisco Bay for a time, he turned to me and said "Unfortunately that is not a concern for PG&E." In the face of his attitude, it was hard for me to feel I would ever have an impact on the corporate world.

However, I was able to support Safeway's next chairman when he resisted efforts on the part of the board to oppose labor unions' demands. Peter McGowan felt the company needed the unions; they were someone to talk to about the competitive challenges facing the company. Even though he was tough on unions, Peter didn't want to break them. I was able to raise several other questions I hoped would help us rethink corporate policy. But frankly, I don't believe I made a contribution to consumers, or to women's rights, or to any other public interest issue I tried to raise.

During this same time, I was elected to the Board of Directors of American Airlines. When I joined Western Union as Vice President for Consumer Affairs, I had given a press interview pointing out that telecommunications enabled companies and non-profits as well as individuals to exchange information electronically and also enabled companies to set up video conferencing that competed with the more traditional forms of transportation like airlines, railroads and buses. That interview proved to have interesting repercussions when I sat on the board of American Airlines.

This was an interesting time for the nation's airlines. They were at the center of the country's first major deregulation push. Dr. Alfred Kahn, economist from Cornell University, was appointed by President Carter to be the first deregulation Tsar. Alfred Casey, board chair of American Airlines, was strongly opposed to deregulation, and at the same time, was making speeches around the country touting the importance of competition. I thought the two positions were inconsistent and said so to him at one of our board meetings. He was furious.

I explained I thought American Airlines should be prudent and prepared to take whatever advantages it could if Congress voted for deregulation. This meant to me that, whatever the company said privately, it should begin to analyze its own business situation and determine the type of regulation that would be most compatible with the company's airline routes. Casey viewed this as treason and from one of his own directors!

I also took issue with American Airline's advertising. They had mounted an ad campaign showing a young woman on the beach under the caption "Get Out in the Sun and Bake. Fly American." I wasn't the only woman who protested. Several women stockholders appeared at one of the stockholder meetings and complained that the ad was demeaning to women.

Bob Crandall, Vice President of Marketing, who later became president of the company, had developed this ad campaign. When I protested the sexist nature of the ad, he laughed and said, "You should see the response it draws, Mary." It was Crandall's cynical way of pointing to the positive impact of the ad. All of this undoubtedly built up in Al Casey's mind. When I came to the next board of director's meeting in Dallas, Texas, he said my position at Western Union was a conflict of interest with my board membership. He asked for my resignation. This was not an issue I wanted to fight. I resigned.

As often happens in life, my resignation from the American Airlines board had some interesting consequences. Lew Waserman, chair of the board of the Music Corporation of American (MCA) which owned Universal Pictures, among other things, also sat on the American Airlines Board. Just as I was the only woman on the board, Lew was the only Jew, and the two of us were the only Democrats. Several times during board meetings we would swap stories about LBJ. Obviously, Lew's stories were more personal and voluminous than mine since he was a long time friend of President Johnson's, and was on the board of the LBJ foundation. Lew was also a major contributor to the Democratic Party and I believe, was one of the earliest supporters of LBJ when he was just a young Congressman from Texas.

Shortly after my resignation from American Airlines, Lew invited me to his New York office. I had always heard that the most powerful executives have clean desks. That was particularly true of Lew. His was spotless. And he was one of the most powerful corporate leaders in the country. He asked me to be a member of the MCA board, and told me he thought I would have a lot of fun. I happily accepted his invitation. His board was a powerhouse.[1]

I felt like a fish out of water and was certainly out of my depths. I didn't play golf in Palm Springs, nor did I cruise on my yacht in the Caribbean, or play the ponies. But above all, I wasn't experienced with the high finance of the corporate world. I was never quite comfortable on the board, but I liked the board members individually and felt respected by them. However, Lew was the dominant figure, and I couldn't imagine any of us confronting him head on during a board meeting. He was the type of executive who ruled with an iron fist in a velvet glove. However, Lew was sensitive to his board and one of the most gracious people I have ever met. I also suspect that if any director had a problem about MCA, they talked it over privately with Lew.

Midway into my term on the MCA board, Lew suggested that they institute a modest board retirement plan. I remember at the time saying to Bob Schwartz how much that retirement benefit would mean to me. Bob looked at me and said, "I am sure Lew understood that when he made his proposal." He was probably right. A $25,000 retirement benefit would have had little meaning to most of the board members, who were corporate executives and earning high salaries, but it would mean a lot to directors like me.

I liked Bob Schwartz. With all the power he amassed over a lifetime, he never felt comfortable in the stretch limousines MCA would send to meet us at the LA airport. He asked for a smaller, less conspicuous car. I joined him in that request and we frequently shared the car on our trips back and forth to the airport. During these trips, he would regale me with stories about his early life. He loved to talk and I loved to listen. He told me about his children, who never understood how it was that he and his wife had so much to say to each other after so many years of marriage.

He also told me that when he was young, his earliest ambition was to be an executive in Houston's United Way. He went to work for the organization as a young staffer, and was disturbed by the way the United Way funds were being distributed within the community. He told me they didn't appreciate having suggestions from a little "Jew boy" and he was summarily fired.

Years later, when he worked on John Connelly's campaign for Governor and Connelly was elected, Connelly asked him what position he wanted. Bob said he wanted to be involved in the governor's political appointments. He then recommended several prominent Jewish scholars and rabbis to the University of Texas Board of Regents. That was not a message that was missed by his earlier United Way bosses.

On our trips back and forth between the LA airport and MCA headquarters at Universal Studios, Bob would be on the car telephone. He said if he ever lost touch with people or if people no longer called him, he would feel he was nothing. I could understand that feeling because my public life had meant an enormous amount to me and I missed it after I left the FTC. I found I had to work very hard if I wanted to stay in the public eye and get their attention. After Lew sold MCA to the Japanese, I resigned from the board. But Lew was right. The company had been a lot of fun!

I also sat on the John Wiley Publishing Company board that was very interesting. Unfortunately, it was suggested that my Wiley directorship was thought to be a conflict of interest with my MCA board membership so I resigned from Wiley. One of my favorite boards was the Alcon Pharmaceutical Corporation. It was smaller, its members were less powerful figures, and the regulatory issues pharmaceutical companies were confronting were more directly oriented to the consumer needs and concerns I was familiar with. It was here I felt I really had something to contribute. It was on this board that the directors spent an enormous amount of time trying to persuade the remaining founder to step down. He had been grooming his successor for almost twenty years but it was poignant watching that man struggle with what he knew he ought to do and actually letting go. In the end, he couldn't bear to turn it over to his successor and sold the company to a foreign pharmaceutical company who promptly made the young man its president and solely responsible for the North American market.

My board directorships were an interesting experience and I am happy I held them in what was then a much simpler time. I knew my qualifications for board membership were based on the fact I was a woman, my sensitivity to consumers and my regulatory savvy. But I was not able to make a dent on the basic financial and business marketing orientation of any of my fellow board members.

One of the personal benefits I got from my corporate experience, was the opportunity it gave me to see Doug in Los Angeles and Charlie and Lynne in Davis, California. After Abby's death, Lynne had moved to the University of California at Davis to enroll in a master's program in plant pathology. Charlie joined her, so I had the opportunity to see them almost every two months during our Safeway board cycle. They took me on my first camping trip, and we also spent many happy days exploring the wine country in Napa Valley outside San Francisco.

While at Western Union, I had continued to travel around the country giving speeches about consumer issues. Slowly, my thinking evolved and I began to consider seriously ways I could help to make consumers' interests more of a decision making force in the country. I had stressed this as I spoke to consumer groups and when speaking to business, I urged them to consider the impact of their decisions on the larger community, stressing the importance of viewing consumers in a broader context not solely as customers.

But still I found that neither Western Union nor my board memberships gave me the same sense of meaning that my public service career had given me. Although I was intellectually challenged by my job at Western Union, I was never emotionally involved. I found it difficult to get excited about helping Western Union to be competitive and more sensitive to its customers. My heart was still in the consumer movement and speaking about consumer issues was not enough. I wanted very much to be involved in a more active capacity than I was able to be at Western Union.

So after seven years, my pension vested and in 1982 when I turned 62, I took early retirement and returned to my first love, the consumer movement.

Notes

1. Members included Bob Schwartz, senior partner of the law firm of Akin and Gump, former Democratic Committee Chair and later ambassador to the USSR, Howard Allen, Chairman of the Board of Southern Gas and Electric, Tom Jones, Chairman of the Board of Northrup Corporation and Felix Rohaten, Senior Partner of Lazar Freres and more recently financial advisor to New York City.

Consumers' Champion

My view of the consumer movement was an affirmative one. I wanted a movement that would reflect and represent consumer interests in the total environment and would focus on consumer opportunities. I passionately believed we needed to give voice to consumers' larger interests in the economy, the environment, and energy management, and do more than just highlight faulty products, deceptive sales practices, and other corporate misdeeds. I felt we should be visionary and focus our energies on the emerging telecommunications technologies that promised more effective ways for consumers to access important consumer services: health care, banking, investment and information and communications services. Also these new technologies offered consumers unique ways of acquiring their own customized information that could be tailored to meet their own specific needs.

Equally exciting was the possibility of new, two-way video with mounted camera to enable families to see and be seen and talk with their friends and other family members, whether on the next block or a continent away. Most important, in my view, was for consumers to see and talk with their health care professionals via television, and avoid seniors having to find transportation for routine visits to their doctors, or young parents having to bundle up their families in the middle of the night to visit the emergency room. The new opportunities were vast and exciting and needed direct consumer input.

I firmly believed that now, more than ever, it was essential that the interests of the consumer-citizen be viewed on a par with the business and labor interests that operate in our society. I was convinced that a reconstituted consumer movement had the potential to be a countervailing force against our country's entrenched centers of corporate power that seemed to grow stronger every day. But consumers needed to organize and focus their combined energies on these broader societal issues. The more I thought about it the more excited I became. My question was, what could be done and what could I do to make it happen.

I spent many hours talking with my friend and consumer colleague, Helen Nelson. She had been appointed consumer advocate by California Governor Edmund "Pat" Brown and was charged with defining consumer needs and interests in California. Very early, we recognized that the marketplace must not be the sole area of consumer concern; our lives were being directly impacted by issues of inflation, housing, energy, pollution and health care. A strong consumer movement could have a direct impact on decision-making as the country grappled with these issues.

In early 1978, while I was still with Western Union, Helen and I decided to invite consumer thinkers, humanists, scholars, opinion leaders and activists to a three-day seminar we convened in Woodstock, Illinois. Our invitation stated the purpose of our seminar:

> *To think deeply about our society today, its inadequacies and failures, and the institutional and personal changes which must take place if we are to create the type of compassionate, humanistic and cooperative sharing environment which is a prerequisite for finding solutions to the critical resource and power imbalances which are endemic throughout the world.*

We wanted to develop strategies that would translate consumer interests into an effective force to influence government's development of national policy. The conference was enormously successful. We had an enthusiastic response to our invitation and we found ourselves largely preaching to the choir. Very quickly, we came together and defined this broader, proactive view of consumer interests, and developed strategies to implement our thinking.

A follow-up conference was held in Williamsburg, Virginia eight months later. Again we had an enthusiastic response, and we prepared a

Statement of Principles of Consumer Interest, as well as a proposal to create a non-profit organization that would reflect the ideas generated at these two conferences.

Out of these conferences, the Consumer Interest Research Institute (CIRI) was created and incorporated in 1980. In January 1981, CIRI received its 501(c)(3) tax exemption. With the help of Ruth Jordan, another consumer colleague, advocate and friend, we put together an impressive list of thirty-five supporters from business, labor, academia and the public interest world and asked these high profile people to lend us their support. They eagerly embraced our principles, enthusiastically supported the need for consumer-oriented research that would document consumer interests and agreed to be listed on our publicity materials as CIRI Initiators.[1] We developed a budget that allowed us to have a small staff to design the basic research, information and implementation capabilities we believed the organization needed.

We appointed a board of directors that included activist consumers, academics and environmentalists.[2] The board met quarterly, but its members contributed many hours to brainstorming projects for CIRI, as well as ideas and strategies for fund raising.

With these building blocks in place, and a mission statement adopted, the time was fast approaching when I needed to devote full time to CIRI. I was excited about making CIRI a reality and now I had the major incentive I needed to take early retirement from Western Union. When I left it was, of course, a change, but only from paid to unpaid work. I never viewed it as retirement. I saw it as providing me the emotional satisfaction and autonomy I knew I needed in my working environment.

My dream was that CIRI would become the Brookings Institute of the consumer movement, and be able to provide the necessary long-range action and policy research that few advocates had time to do. But, building CIRI turned out to be more difficult than I had imagined. The timing was not propitious. President Reagan and the Republicans were coming to power. Almost immediately, the new administration set about dismantling a wide range of social programs created by the Johnson administration, as well as the agencies that had been established to implement them. This was hardly the time for a new public interest organization, when many of those already under contract to these government agencies felt the pinch of the Republican cutbacks.

We made the rounds of all the major foundations that had been active in funding the start-up of many social action non-profit organizations during the '60s and '70s. We were seeking seed money to get CIRI started and always received the most cordial reception from the various foundation executives we talked with. They were interested in our concept and asked many questions, but we were an utter failure in getting them to give us the much needed funding.

Universities were an equally hard sell. From the beginning, I felt the best home for CIRI might be as an institute within a major university; there we could access their best minds and simultaneously draw on their fund raising capabilities. What I learned the hard way was that universities expected institutes to secure their own funding, and universities then took a healthy cut, so this was hardly a fruitful tree to pluck!

Slowly, it became clear to us that start-up funds for CIRI were not available and the half million-dollar budget we had proposed was not going to happen. Furthermore, I simply didn't have the salesmanship skills to pull it off. I could generate substantial enthusiasm and respect from potential donors, but in the last analysis I couldn't close the sale. Nor did I have the savvy to engage others to help me do this fund raising. The next question, then, became where do we go from here and what could I do to make CIRI a reality?

I did manage to raise some money from individual business contacts I had made in my earlier career and also from personal friends that allowed us to keep going with a part time secretary, and me working, full time, pro bono. I negotiated with law firms to contribute my expertise in exchange for office space for CIRI. This was the extent of what I found I was able to do. It was not enough. In the end, I painfully discovered I was not a successful salesperson. I loved the policy discussions, but I never did learn how to close the sale. I wasn't clever enough to come away with a check or even a promise to look more closely into the need for an organization such as CIRI.

Together with the board we decided on another strategy. We kept our head above water by developing a variety of projects that began the slow but arduous process of building the necessary CIRI infrastructure to gain visibility, and develop a track record.

In 1983, when Social Security and Medicare were going through one of their periodic crises, CIRI's first funded project was a conference on defining consumers' interests, since one of the solutions being proposed focused on cutting back on consumer benefits. The CIRI conference, funded by the MacArthur and Sloan Foundations, dealt with strategies to meet the "crisis" without reducing those benefits. The conference was successful and resulted in the publication of a videocassette, "Taking the Long View: Social Security and Medicare," accompanied by a study guide illuminating consumer policy issues. We distributed these as an educational tool to various community organizations: libraries, school systems, business, labor, as well as to state and local government departments of aging. We also tried to sell these materials to the general public, but were only able to generate $1000 in revenues.

Pursuing my longtime interest in introducing consumers to the new telecommunications technologies, my board agreed on several projects to further this goal. We put on a day and a half workshop to demonstrate to community leaders the value and potential relevance of these telecomputer services to their work. We pointed out how these technologies would make their work easier, faster and cheaper, and enable their services to reach a much wider audience. We published a pamphlet based on the results of the workshop and on a number of the interviews we had conducted with non-profit organizations already using these technologies.[3] Once again, the workshop was a success, and the pamphlet found its niche, but it didn't help us to raise money.

In 1990, CIRI joined with the Institute of Alternative Futures, a think tank in Virginia, to present a conference on the health care services that could be promoted and delivered electronically. Telemedicine, as this new health care development was called, became a consuming passion of mine, and for many years I wrote articles and gave speeches publicizing the broad range of home-based health services that could be made available electronically to consumers in their homes.[4] I was invited to speak at the annual meetings of the Telemedicine Association and by hospitals and other health care organizations who saw telemedicine as a way for them to improve their patients' access to health care.

At that time, Vice President Al Gore and other policy makers were promoting these high-speed networks, but they were focused primarily on building them in and between communities to connect hospitals and health clinics in urban and rural areas. Mine was the lone voice for some time stressing the need to connect these networks directly into the home. I wanted to ensure that consumers could contact their doctors and health care professionals directly in the middle of the night, and not have to bundle up their families and go to the emergency room, and that young mothers could bring their premature infants home much earlier with the comfort and security of being in instant two-way video contact with their doctors. The concept of home-care applications for this technology has now been accepted, but the cable and telephone networks still have not installed the type of wiring necessary to make it possible for homeowners to receive two-way video and voice communications into and out of their homes.

I believe CIRI made a real contribution. I was pleased that at one of the Telemedicine Association's annual conferences, my work to promote these technologies to the home was applauded and publicly recognized. But CIRI's work was too closely associated with my personal activities and that of the other board members. As a result, we were not making the necessary progress to establish CIRI as an independent functioning entity.

I learned to appreciate the wise and thoughtful advice of the board members; CIRI could not have managed without them, but I'm not sure I appreciated that at the time. I had a grand vision, and didn't want to settle for smaller more practical moves such as a newsletter. I regarded that as fluff, and thought it contributed little to the knowledge base. Looking back, I was probably too stiff-necked. Putting out a newsletter would have forced me to focus on what I thought CIRI should do. Also, it would have given CIRI some visibility and purpose in the public's mind.

As CIRI was winding down, I was traveling more and took advantage of this breathing space to visit my nephew, David, who was then living in London. David and I went back a long way, when I used to take him into New York to go to the various shooting galleries scattered along Broadway; or when we were both in Cold Spring Harbor, taking him and his friend, Donald Ferris in my red Triumph to the movies. When the Vietnam war broke out, David was the only family member who volunteered to go into the armed services. He was married to Eileen Gloger at the time, and went to the Harvard Business School after the war ended. He made his career in investment banking, joined Goldman Sachs, and was soon sent to London, where he and Eileen brought up their two children, Marc and Sharon.

Sadly, their marriage ended in divorce, and in 1980, when Abby got married, this was the last occasion when they all, as a family, came over to attend. David was subsequently remarried to Patti Archer, and they continued to live in London, with Marc and Sharon dividing their time between David and Patti, and Eileen, who continued her psychotherapy practice in London. David is a wonderfully kind person and always generous when others are in need. He and Patti now have a third son, Christopher, whom I do not know as well because they lived so long in London, and only recently returned to the states.

While I was struggling with CIRI's growing up, I was also struggling with some growing up of my own. Betty was still in Washington and widowed. Jim had died prematurely and she was having a difficult time adjusting to the loss of a lovable man who adored her. When Jim died, she no longer had that anchor to help her deal with the inner turmoil we all shared as a result of our troubled childhood.

Betty was always enormously supportive of me during my psychoanalysis and during my fight with Ann. I think I failed Betty badly when Jim died, as I just didn't appreciate what a loss that was to her. Things periodically would get difficult between Betty and me. I felt she was irritated with me and I didn't know how to cope with that other than to get angry. I knew we loved each other but the tension was always there. My issues with Betty made me realize that, once again. I needed professional help to help me work through these conflicts.

I found a psychologist and began seeing her once a week. As I tried to work out how I could change my sister's attitude toward me, it finally dawned on me I could not change another person and that I needed to change myself! I learned to accept Betty, as she was, a widow who was suffering without the necessary tools to deal with her grief. As I worked through my feelings towards Betty and began to recognize her needs and not just my own, we slowly entered into a closer and more adult relationship. I'm grateful for that.

It was also during this period that I realized something important about CIRI. I had been talking with a friend of mine, a novelist and an organizational development consultant, who asked me what a good day at CIRI would look like. Enthusiastically I began describing the day. As I talked on, I realized I was describing a day at the FTC. I had never let go of those heady years and I wondered, for the first time, if that had been one of my major motivations in creating CIRI in the first place. It was a significant realization for me and with it some of my enthusiasm for CIRI cooled. I kept going, but I no longer had the same drive.

In March 2000, I finally bit the bullet. I had talked with the board about ways to keep CIRI going. We talked of merging with another consumer organization but couldn't identify one where the fit was right. At the time, I was president of the Mental Health Association of the District of Columbia (MHA D.C.), and had written a Children's Resource Directory, "Keep Your Kids Healthy Mentally." MHA D.C. was about to launch a public awareness campaign to promote the understanding of mental illness as a brain disorder. These projects were directed at consumers and providers of mental health services who shared a deep concern about citizen access to mental health services.

I suggested to the CIRI board that perhaps we should consider turning over our assets to MHA D.C. CIRI had accumulated $60,000, a substantial sum, but not sufficient to pay for either an office or one staff person. The board liked the idea of CIRI's resources being applied to issues concerning children but was concerned that in any transfer, CIRI's major consumer oriented research mission might get lost.

Above all, they wanted to be sure that a transfer of CIRI funds would not be a one-shot deal for MHA D.C. They wanted the money to be used as seed money in building a consumer research program, and to see some acknowledgement of CIRI in the history of MHA D.C., perhaps in the form of a specific project. With these stipulations, they voted unanimously that MHA D.C. would be an appropriate beneficiary of CIRI's funds and they directed me to move ahead with transferring them, and simultaneously, with dissolving CIRI. Today, MHA D.C. has a research program that it has named the Consumer Interest Research Program that made its first grants in 2005.

Abandoning the concept and reality of CIRI was not easy for me. It marked a major change in my life from managing an organization to learning how to become a volunteer with its much more amorphous responsibilities, and the stigma that society attaches to a volunteer, as contrasted with a highly-paid executive.

Notes

1. They included John Gardner, former Secretary of Health and Human Welfare Department and then president of Common Cause; Robert Heilbroner, economist and professor at New York's New School of Social Research; Harlan Cleveland, founding dean, University of Minnesota's Hubert Humphrey Institute of Public Affairs; Robert Nathan, new deal economist and CEO, Nathan Associates in DC; Esther Peterson, Women's Bureau of the Department of Labor, and LBJ's Consumer Representative; Andrew Brimmer, director, Federal Reserve Board; Jacob Clayman, Ladies Garment Worker Union; William Dyson, author and management expert; Victor Gotbaum, president, Municipal Employees Union in New York; Michael Pertshuk, former chair of the Federal Trade Commission; Hazel Henderson, environmentalist; David Finn, president. Ruder and Finn and Caroline Ware, dean of the consumer movement;

2. Helen Nelson, chair, Ruth Jordan, Esther Peterson, Caroline Ware, Nancy Chasen, writer, Dennis Pirages, environmental professor, Monroe Friedman, professor of Consumer Economics, and myself.

3. *The Potential of Telecommunications for Non Profit Organizations—Everything You Were Never Told About Using Your Computer, TV & Telephone for High Impact Communications,* (1989) co-authored by Nancy Chasen and myself.

4. "The New Information Technologies and Consumer Choice," with Helen Nelson, *Proceedings of the Second International Conference on Research in the Consumer Interest* (1990); "Healthcare For An Aging America: The Role of Telecommunications," 2021 A.D. Visions of Society, Technology and Communications Forum, at the Conform Information Networking National Engineering Consortium (1991);" Electronic House Calls: 21st Century Options"(1995); "Telemedicine and the National Infrastructure: Are the Realities of the Health Care Being Ignored?," *Journal of the American Medical Informatics Association,* 4, (Nov.-Dec. 1997): p. 399.

Retirement, a Demanding Challenge

When I finally accepted that CIRI was not going to take off, I found myself doing the kind of thinking I should have done before I took early retirement. It hadn't occurred to me when I left Western Union that I was retiring; I thought of it as shifting focus and doing what gave me emotional satisfaction: I viewed CIRI as a new full time job. The only difference was that I wasn't getting paid for the work I wanted to do.

Fortunately, I had enough money to "retire." Ever since college, I have taken great pride in having managed my life without financial help from my family. Except for a small allowance from my uncle during law school, I had taken care of all my own graduate school tuition and living expenses. The lifestyle I had developed for myself—my home, its furnishings, and my travels and entertainment, I had managed on the income I earned. It wasn't until after I left Western Union, and mother and Livy had died, that I inherited some money. I was only too happy to use it to supplement my retirement income, and it enabled me to continue doing the kind of work I had always enjoyed.

Working in retirement was not the same as being a fulltime professional. I had neither the responsibilities I wanted nor the opportunity to be creative and run things. But, most of all, I no longer had a large organization to provide me with an identity. As a fulltime professional with increasing autonomy and authority within the various organizations where I worked, my tendency to be a loner finally gave way to greater collegiality. By the time I left Western Union, I thought I had achieved a kind of balance between my loan wolf and team player personas.

Unfortunately, with CIRI, I realized I missed being part of a larger organization, and I was reluctant to reach out and work as an equal with others who shared my interest. I reverted back to being a loner, at least professionally. When I couldn't make a go of CIRI and found myself retired, I had no group to be a part of, though there was an active consumer movement in the District. What I realize now is that Western Union met my needs to be part of a "family," while at the same time allowing me to be free of any real supervision. I could be "myself," whatever that meant to me at the time.

For me, CIRI was professionally lonely; I wasn't able to develop creative ideas working by myself. Above all, I learned I wasn't a fundraiser, which was a necessary basic skill if CIRI was to survive. Through all the ten years of CIRI, I refused to think of myself as retired. I was negative about retirement and everything I thought it meant: stopping work, playing golf, shopping, going to museums, etc. In my mind that was trivia, none of which appealed to me as something to do full time. Above all, I saw it as a loss of authority and the identity I needed. I needed an outlet for my creativity, and work was the only outlet I knew.

Knowing that CIRI was no longer an option, I struggled with what to do next. I decided to take a Ph.D. at Georgetown University. Once before, in the early 60s, and while still at the FTC, I tried to get a Ph.D. from Georgetown but, true to form, I was oblivious to the fact that candidates were storming the gates of all graduate schools; many probably seeking admission as a way to avoid the draft. I remember arriving on the doorstep of the dean of Georgetown's graduate studies and announcing I wanted to take a Ph.D. in regulatory administrative policy. He looked at me, asked how old I was—I think I was about forty-six at the time—and said I would find it a killing pace while I was an active FTC commissioner. I pooh-poohed the idea but they turned me down! Looking back on that process now I laugh at my arrogance, but at the time I was outraged. This time, when I approached Georgetown, I played the role of supplicant. I think they were fascinated by the idea of a seventy-year old taking a Ph.D. I was admitted.

I loved the classes and thoroughly enjoyed my fellow students. The professors, mostly from the Vietnam generation, were often anti- government. I expounded on what a wonderful experience public service had been for me. Once, I remember telling one of my political science classes with great enthusiasm that one of my proudest moments in my law career was when I was able to go into court as a chief government attorney, rise to my feet and announce to the judge, we were "ready for the United States Government." I don't think the students knew what I was talking about, nor had they ever heard anyone talking about public service in quite that way. Hopefully, it made an impression and maybe some of them even considered entering government service, but I don't know that.

Pursuing a Ph.D. was an interesting experience, but not as exciting as I had hoped. Part of my problem was that too many of the fields I was interested in—such as health care and social welfare policy—had prerequisites that required statistics or something similar, and I was afraid I couldn't do that. So I settled for a more traditional doctoral program in political science with fewer difficult prerequisites. Most of the courses I took were mundane, and I realized, at seventy-plus, it was harder for me to learn and certainly it was harder for me to retain the material.

I did manage to complete all the course work, fulfilled the German and French language requirements, and passed the comprehensive exam that I had failed on my first try, due in part to my political naivete. There was a question that focused on whether systemic conditions or the leadership of individuals most affected change. I argued it was individuals. This was not well received by the political science professors, who believed the system was all-important. After all, that was their discipline. I had also failed to back up my views with sufficient research. I made sure not to make that same mistake again.

The second time, they passed me. But I never did finish my thesis as I found I no longer wanted to do that kind of research. I liked writing articles and speeches and doing some research, but not in the depth required for a doctoral thesis.

After two years in graduate school, I was still floundering and toyed briefly with getting a fulltime job. I joined a weekend workshop on how to find employment after retirement. They asked us to fill out various questionnaires about what we had liked about our various jobs, which made me think about my work as different challenges rather than as what a lawyer or corporate executive did. It forced me to think about myself in a different way, not just as a lawyer but also as someone who wanted to take charge, be creative, and who definitely wanted work that was meaningful. I began to think about my skills as generic that could be applied to a broad range of jobs, and I began to think of areas where I might like to work.

But in the end, I wasn't able to confront the job market. Still scarred from my earlier job-hunting experiences, I wasn't willing to reach out and confront the possibility of rejection. I needed only eighteen months more in the government workforce to qualify for a full retirement benefit, but the thought of looking there was too difficult for me.

So I involved myself in different volunteer activities, and explored my desire to be more connected with people and society. I began to reach out, make new friends, and most important, learned to spend time with them. I joined a group of sixteen senior citizens who were interested in issues facing older Americans. We are still together. We meet once a month and call ourselves the Vital Aging Group. At each meeting we "check in" and report briefly on what has happened to us during the preceding month, then exchange thoughts and share our musings on retirement. The friendships are precious.

I also started to reach out more to my family and we have become much closer. My nephew, David, invited me to join a group he helped organize. The group meets once a year and discusses public policy issues of concern to its members. It is mainly a men's group though wives do attend and contribute to the discussion. David, more conservative than I, is always thoughtful in his positions and I decided to join because he and I have an important family relationship I want to continue. We had been separated from each other for too long when he lived in London, and I saw joining his policy group as a way to resume our relationship. We have gone to these agenda meetings together for many years and I find them stimulating. It's also wonderful to be sharing something together.

When Ann died in 1994, David said to me, "You are now the older generation." That was a sobering thought but it made me think about my relationship to all my nephews and their families. Now I call them more often and work at keeping in touch with what they are doing. This growing and ongoing relationship with my family is a great joy and a source of deep satisfaction.

David's son, Marc, attended Cornell University and while still an undergraduate got involved in managing a scholastic testing service at the college. Like his father, Marc was business-oriented and after college, he went into an investment house; first on Wall Street, and later he went to Boston with a venture capital firm. After a few years, he went on to do graduate work in the Columbia Business School and married Sarah, a girl from Denmark, who, I believe, was homesick and had trouble adjusting to the States. Unfortunately, the marriage didn't last although they both tried hard to make it work. Marc now is in real estate and developing shopping centers in low-income neighborhoods. He has achieved his desire to do good, as well as doing very well.

In 1994, Marc's sister, Sharon, returned to the states to look at colleges. Naturally, I was delighted when she chose American University in Washington D.C. I helped her move into the freshman dorm and kept in touch with her as she began her college life. It was wonderful for me. I loved Sharon and had known her as a little girl when they lived in London and they would come to Nantucket for the summer. Sharon also visited me in Washington when she was about ten or eleven, and introduced me to my first pizza. One summer, when Helen Nelson and I went to Paris for a summer vacation, Sharon came along. She was about fourteen and the last thing she wanted to do was to sightsee! Her goal was to find a particular kind of mini skirt that was all the rage in London, so we let her go her way as we went ours.

Sharon found the differences between her English background and that of her American classmates confusing; she found many of the students superficial and interested primarily in partying and dating. Now, once again and with a new generation, my house became a refuge when the going was difficult. I gave her a key to the house so she could come and go as she pleased. At times, while attending classes, she would stay with me for several days at a time.

But for me, once again I had to learn how to be with another person I was close to and accept their love. I needed help to cope. I chose my familiar route and went back into therapy with my former analyst, Henry Siegel. We had a history together so we didn't have to spend time on my background and emotional life. As always in analysis, the problem turned out to be more about me than the other person. My insecurity and poor self-image reared its ugly head and created great anxiety and feelings of inadequacy.

Henry helped me relate to Sharon, as I sincerely wanted to do, and helped me stop second-guessing another person. He taught me Sharon was capable of telling me when I was being intrusive, and he was right. I found that one of the things I loved about Sharon was her willingness to tell me to get off her back when she felt I was interfering. I learned to appreciate this, and her ability to do this made me feel more secure in just being myself. Today Sharon is a very successful professional. After earning her Master of Arts in international communications at American University, she worked at the World Bank, has made several field trips with them and is currently deciding what her next steps should be.

As the years have gone by, and while my family has become increasingly important to me, I found that my closeness to them could not be at the expense of an independent life. The feeling of independence is vital to my well-being. I had ruled out going back into the work force and the only option I could see was to explore the volunteer world. I was invited to join the board of the Older Women's League and at the suggestion of my nephew, John, I contacted Anita Shelton, executive director of the D.C. Mental Health Association. He and Anita had both worked for the D.C. Office of Human Rights. John thought with my interest in mental health, it might be worthwhile to investigate what was going on there and see if this might be an avenue for my skills and energies. He turned out to be very perceptive.

John had spent most of his adult life in the African-American world working for the Woodrow Wilson Institute and the Urban League. After he received his social work degree from Howard University, he became a psychiatric social worker and practiced at St Elizabeth's Mental Health Hospital in the District.

John is particularly empathetic to the interests and concerns of African-Americans, and has opened his home as a refuge for many who need a friend or mentor. Also, he is talented at design and building, and restored an old Victorian house in northeast Washington that belonged to his brother, David. His work has been cited in the magazine of the National Historic Trust, a rare honor for a restoration novice. John is a gifted therapist; but, like so many others, he found it difficult to confront the realities of the Medicaid and HMO reimbursement systems. He decided he couldn't practice under these conditions, so he quit his job in D.C. and moved to Pennsylvania.

Meanwhile, I continued to pursue my volunteer activities. Working with colleagues who had access to both funds and technical recources, several of us got together in the 1980s to promote the public's understanding of how the new telecommunications networks could serve their information and service needs. We co-founded another public interest organization which we called the Alliance for Public Technology. It is devoted to promoting the delivery of the new technology to consumers, schools and municipalities; enabling them to access the vast new information resources and participate in two way video communications in and out of their homes and classrooms. This is a highly technical field, and it was a challenge for us to translate the technology into understandable terms so the public could understand what these networks could do for them.

It was fun to have colleagues to work with again, and money to fund our ideas.[1] But once again, as president of the organization, I found myself in conflict with the chair of the board over our respective responsibilities. She was already very active in the field and was a professor of communications in a west coast university; certainly she was far more knowledgeable about the field than I. This time I managed to keep my feelings under control, but the experience demonstrated to me my continuing problem dealing with authority, my own, as well as that of other people.

I also joined the board of the D.C. Mental Health Association, and worked on programs to bring counseling services to homeless families living in shelters. In the early 1990s, Anita Shelton left the association to head up another non-profit organization she had organized. After her departure, the association never recovered its active stance. In 1998, the board had to make a decision whether to close the association or try to revive it. I volunteered to take over the presidency. My offer was accepted and thus began my most active career since dissolving CIRI.

My first goal was to raise money. We received a $10,000 grant from the National Institute of Mental Health's Substance Abuse Mental Health Administration (SAMHSA) and set about to develop a directory of children's mental health resources within the District. It was a good project to jump-start the association because we could do it without a paid staff. We developed a directory, "Keep Your Kids Healthy Mentally," and printed 3000 copies. The D.C. Office of Early Child Development agreed to take on the distribution responsibility and the project took off and gave us the track record we needed for other funding.

During my first year as president, we also developed a mental health public awareness campaign funded by what was then the D.C. Commission on Mental Health Services. We received a grant of $20,000, but it was too small to mount a comprehensive program. Fortunately, I found a wonderful young woman, Ruth Giglioti, with solid marketing experience who was ready to start her own business, and was willing to take us on at a substantially reduced fee. She developed a limited but very effective public awareness campaign, "Get a Fresh Outlook on Mental Illness." I ran the association for three years with a part-time administrative assistant, the occasional college intern and help from many of my board members. I was active and loved it.

As the association president, I also became active in many D.C. mental health advocacy groups working to reform the D.C. Commission on Mental Health Services. The Commission was run successively by two court appointed receivers as a result of a lawsuit brought by the D.C. mental health advocates, and MHA D.C. worked with both of these receivers. As president, I formed a coalition of children's mental health advocates and focused my energies on children's services. As a result of the second receiver's leadership, a strong push from the community, and the efforts of the advocates, a new Department of Mental Health was designed and enacted into law by the D.C. City Council.

The second receiver took on the leadership of the new department until he could find a permanent director. We invited him to keynote the association's annual mental health conference. In his speech, he said school mental health services were going to be one of his priorities. After his speech, I contacted him and asked if he would like the Mental Health Association to develop a coalition that could work with him to achieve his goal. He agreed. I put together a great group of family advocates, educators and mental health specialists and we received a modest grant from the Cafritz Foundation to support the coalition's work. We worked with the receiver for more than a year, and succeeded in getting a mental health program introduced into thirty-one schools in the District of Columbia.

We also developed two programs to educate older African-American adults on mental health issues and reached out to black churches and neighborhoods. Funded by the Consumer Health Foundation and Kaiser Family Fund, the program was enthusiastically received and I think the program made some inroads against the stigma and ignorance that so often accompanies mental health issues.

Slowly, the association became a factor in the mental health community and, together with CIRI's money, we were able to hire a full time executive director. It was time for me to let go. I tried not to assert myself as president, but that was difficult for me and, unfortunately, there was little collegiality between the two of us. We were often at loggerheads.

Once again, my experiences in handling authority and my fears about being too dominating created an inordinate anxiety for me, and I sought professional help. This time, I went to a psychiatric social worker who had been recommended to me by a close friend. Her style was different. She saw her role more as a coach to guide me in dealing with the new executive director.

As with the other therapists I had gone to, we spent time talking about my family relationships and my poor self-image. Talking with Harriet about my difficulties, I realized my anxiety once again had roots in my childhood sense of always being in the wrong and doing a "bad" thing if I asserted myself—all shades of mother's teachings about just how a woman should behave. In addition, and equally important, I was still trying to retain control. As I worked through these conflicts, my anxiety dissipated, and I was able to assert myself and voice my disagreements rather than hanging on to them as resentments and just remaining silent.

When my term as president of the Mental Health Association was over, I left the presidency, but stayed on the board. I wanted to continue my advocacy work for the Association and finish another directory we had received funds to prepare, about adult mental health services in the District. However, it became more and more difficult for me, even as a board member, to work with the executive director and the new president, so I decided to resign from the board. I did continue my advocacy work on behalf of children through the children's advocacy and school-based mental health coalitions I had started when I was president.

Advocacy is a challenging experience for me, but I prefer to work for change from the inside, and I worked as much as possible on a colleagial basis with the Department of Mental Health. Unfortunately, my efforts to work with the department did not succeed in initiating the children's services we so desperately needed.

The children's coalition decided to change tactics and go public. As its chair, I prepared a report titled, "Children Deserve The Best." It detailed the Department of Mental Health's failure to develop new service initiatives for children and even to spend the funds budgeted for children's services. When the report was made public, we held a press conference and received substantial coverage in the *Washington Post.* The department's director was furious, but fortunately I had no job in jeopardy. I'm not sure whether our report achieved its goal of creating public pressure for children's services. I do know that as a result of the report, the department discontinued making its budget available in programmatic form, which had enabled us to do the analysis we did.

I volunteered for Hillcrest Children's Center run by my old friend, Anita Shelton, and have rejoined the mental health association's board of directors at the urging of some of its members. My nemesis, the past executive director, is no longer there. The association is trying to make a comeback. It has elected a new president and hired a new executive director and I wanted to help where I can. After a year, the board invited me to resume the presidency, which I agreed to do—still optimistic that we could make the association an important factor in D.C.'s mental health system. I have an excellent active board and I am determined to work closely with them to develop the programs and financing we so desperately need.

As a culmination of my mental health work, I sought out and was invited to be a member of the Institutional Review Board of the National Institute of Mental Health (NIMH). The board's responsibility is to evaluate the impact of proposed research on the human subjects involved in the research. This was a new and exciting challenge for me.

I sat as a community member of the board but I found the scientist members were more sensitive to, and understood better, the proposed treatments and possible adverse impact on research subjects. My concerns were to ensure that the research participants fully understood their confidentiality and privacy rights, and to try to persuade my fellow review board members to require that the data they collect about the different ethnic and minority groups involved in the research projects be retained and analyzed wherever feasible. In my view, it is essential to insure that this data be available to future researchers who might be interested in studying the impact of mental health drugs on different ethnic and minority groups. In general, I found the NIMH Review Board work highly technical and I didn't feel I had the background or stature to make any real contribution so I resigned after several years.

The volunteer experience is an interesting one. I certainly hadn't planned on being a volunteer in my old age. I don't think I seriously thought about it. But I have found that one of the major differences between volunteering and paid work is the more precise definition of authority and responsibilities existing in the paid professional world.

I always knew what my job was at the various law firms, at the FTC and especially at Western Union. It was clear to me to whom I reported and who worked for me. This isn't true in the non-profit world. Many of my difficulties in the volunteer non-profit world stemmed from the ill-defined roles for the presidents, board chairs and executive directors. Given my propensity to take over, I found this ambiguity difficult to deal with. I didn't have the necessary self-confidence to raise the issue proactively and then allow the board to decide the relative responsibilities. I think I have finally mastered some of these challenges. Once again with the help of therapy, I am beginning to understand the importance of leadership, but with control of myself rather than of my colleagues.

What is also important to me is that the obstacles and difficulties I have had as an executive in this non-profit world haven't defeated me. I can thank analysis for that because earlier in my career I am quite sure I would never have been able to survive the various setbacks and anxieties I encountered as I struggled to learn how to continue to be active *and* give up control.

Life continues to be fulfilling and rewarding.

Notes

1. Our money came from membership, subscriptions to our newsletter, and a few foundations. Sam had good contacts with the telephone companies who were generous supporters whose interests coincided with ours in expanding and updating their networks to carry the new communications technologies into business and the home.

Abby Penfield Watkins Bernon, Ann's only daughter and my beloved niece, killed in an automobile accident on Sept. 5, 1980.

Abby and Douglas Bernon three months before she was killed.

The Jones sisters: Mary, Ann and Betty.

Ann and her four boys (from left to right): Charlie, John, Rob and David.

Charlie and Lynne with their daughter, Kelly.

Mary's nephew David Watkins (center) and his family Pati, Marc, Sharon and Christopher.

Mary's nephew, Rob and his wife Susanna with their daughter, Hannah.

Mary's 60th reunion at Wellesley College.

Sue Whitman and Mary in the Dali Museum in Spain.

Mary's bridge partners, Sue Whitman, Florence Boyd, Mary and Georgia Fitzpatrick.

Mary sailing with Charlie's family in the Carribean.

Mary riding bike given to her on her 75th birthday by Charlie and Lynne.

A BACKWARD GLANCE

To know how to grow old is the masterwork of wisdom and one of the most difficult chapters in the Great Art of Living
H. AMIEL, 1874

Through my years of therapy I have learned a lot about myself and how I relate to others. To borrow from Edith Wharton's title to her autobiography, it is time now to take "A Backward Glance" at my experiences in a man's world and my growth as a woman.

Aging has given me a perspective on who I am and where I came from. Thanks to my years in analysis, I am better able to cope with my emotional demons, become a feeling person and live with myself as I am and not yearn for the things that I am not. I take more time to listen. It's easier now for me to express my love for other people and, perhaps more importantly, accept their love in return. In most respects, aging has proved to be a joyful period in my life.

Sadly, however, with age there also comes loss: the deaths of my beloved niece Abby, my two sisters, Betty and Ann, my uncle Livy, and no longer is there a "sense of place." Our family home in Cold Spring Harbor was sold after Ann died in 1994. Her four sons had left Long Island long ago and neither Betty nor I were interested in uprooting ourselves from Washington. Still, it was difficult to see it go out of the family. It was one of the few homes in the country that had remained in the hands of a single family since before the American Revolution.

At the time of the sale the local newspaper quoted Rob, Ann's youngest son, as saying, "It was a difficult decision. Our family to a large extent had derived their identity from that house and from the history of the family with which it had so long been associated. We feel a stewardship role as opposed to an ownership role."

Ann's oldest son, John, took a different tack. He said, "We have to cherish the things that have been accomplished without holding on to them. People shrivel up when they hang on to the past. If they can look back on it with pride and joy and let it go, they are the better for it."

I agree with both of them. We have a proud family history, but we don't need to hang on to its symbols to be sensitive to it. However, one thing is certain; the sale of the family home marks the end of the Jones dynasty. I am the last of the Joneses to bear the family name and when I die the name disappears with me. But the family, with its culture and tradition, lives on through Ann's sons: John, David, Charlie, Rob and their families.

With age I find I'm better able to appreciate where I came from without being swallowed up by it. Also, I accept that psychoanalysis had its major impact on my professional life because, even in that trusting environment, and despite the skill of my therapists, I was never able to talk in any depth about my social relationships. Still, I learned a lot about myself; how I relate to others, what my family and its history meant to me, and especially my role and growth as a woman.

From my earliest childhood, my mother's idea of what it meant to be a woman was deeply ingrained in my psyche: be a wife! Her constant criticism of my appearance was to teach me how I must look to attract boys. Because I wore glasses she would quote the wit, Dorothy Parker, "Boys don't make passes at girls who wear glasses," or because I did well in school, "Don't ever let a boy think you are smarter than he is." In her view, what a girl needed to do to catch a man was flirt and play up to a man's ego. My total education about sex was limited to a series of "don'ts." "Don't pet, Mary. If a boy wants to pet remember he is interested in only one thing. Wait until you get married." Never was there a discussion about the "one thing." Instead it was a series of warnings and admonitions to instill fear.

Mother never made any great pretense of loving father and I could never see what they had in common. Anna L. Jones was a product of her times; marriage was an obligatory state for women and love had little to do with it. In my mother's and grandmother's day, proper women didn't have careers. Marriage was the only avenue open to well brought up women that allowed them to leave the house where they had been born. It gave them the imprimateur to lead enjoyable and secure lives. It was totally a man's world.

When I chose a legal career I went against the grain of my family's preachments and, in their mind, was following a pattern established by my rejected suffragist aunt, Rosalie. Sadly, when I started practicing law, I was professionally lonely. I didn't have female colleagues and I was psychologically incapable of reaching out to other women. I never did look up the few women who were in law school with me, most of whom were married. Because I was single, I felt different and estranged from their social environment and I also never joined the local New York Bar Association or the Woman's Bar. I isolated myself. Work was my life as well as my salvation. Life to me was always around the corner and it wasn't until my analysis that I started to realize I was entitled to a home whether single or married.

Being the "only," or "first" woman in whatever profession or business I was in always made me feel uncomfortable. I didn't feel like a pioneer, I felt like a stranger and didn't want to make waves. I wanted to be treated as an equal but it never occurred to me to challenge the customs or attitudes in the predominately male world where I worked. I just wanted to be let in. I accepted and bought into the male view of women and rarely questioned why there were so few women in key leadership positions. I accepted that women who taught would teach in secondary schools or, if they had advanced degrees, would teach at women's colleges where they were welcomed on the faculty. I knew many 'spinsters' on the Wellesley faculty who were vibrant, intelligent and fulfilled as women. Subconsciously, I think they were the role models for my life.

I found male-oriented language demeaning. To be in a meeting and referred to as "Gentlemen," as if I wasn't there, was abrasive, but in the beginning I said nothing. I found the different vocabularies used to describe successful men and women annihilating. Successful men were "confident," "take charge," and "committed." Successful women were "bossy," "aggressive," and "emotional."[1] I recognize now this reflected deeply ingrained attitudes and not just superficial linguistic expressions;

but they were vocabularies that I put up with. In my day, the greatest compliment a man could give a successful woman was to say she had a mind like a man. I had my share of those compliments and I accepted them without question! Despite my professional achievements I always felt like a fish out of water. I was a loner and felt inferior in social situations because I was single. And I was a woman in conflict.

Looking back from the perspective of age, I recognize that being single had a greater impact on me than I ever admitted to myself. I think many people who knew me wondered why I never married though they recognized I was leading a successful professional life. Like most women, I wanted to have a satisfactory emotional life and a successful career but psychologically, I wasn't able to manage the intimacy that living with another person demanded. On some level I believed that marriage was not possible because I was a professional woman, even though I knew there were many women who managed that duality in their lives.

Looking back, I find it interesting that I maintained this attitude towards men pretty much during my entire life. I had one very serious love affair when I was in my 30s. But typical of most of my relationships with men, those whom I could let myself love were always married, so they were "safe." I didn't have to face the loss of independence that I associated with marriage and had so feared throughout my life.

I was terrified of close relationships and convinced I would get lost; I would either be too dependent or incapable of expressing my needs in a non-confrontational manner. When men approached me seriously, I panicked and fled. Underneath it all, I wondered what was wrong with me because I couldn't manage to sustain a relationship.

In analysis I began to sort out some of these myths and fears. In the beginning I shied away from certain words; I couldn't use the word femininity, for example, it had too many frightening overtones. But slowly I came to grips with my emotions. I recognized I had never personally experienced closeness or love as a child, nor had I ever seen a loving relationship between my mother and father. I associated marriage with problems and interminable fights over money. Gradually, I learned the effect my family's relationships had on me, especially the male role models of a passive father and an adored homosexual uncle. Slowly, I began to unravel my fears of closeness and intimacy, and understand more about my views of marriage. Also, I suspect that part of my feelings of being an outsider came from my family's belief in their superiority and their aloofness from those they didn't consider their social "equals."

As a result of analysis I no longer think of myself as aberrational because I didn't conform to my mother's version of a woman's accepted role. Much of my sense of isolation has disappeared. I have learned to like myself more, and happily have found I can like women and have them as close friends. I have more in common with them than I realized. I recognize there is nothing incompatible between being a professional woman and marriage. But life styles become a habit. After so many years of living alone, it is too difficult to share my life with someone else.

Analysis also enabled me to be a fully productive human being and to enjoy the fascinating people I was lucky enough to encounter along the way. It enabled me to play a small role in making the world a better place. Who else could have had an opportunity to work closely with Wild Bill Donovan, the most committed and creative person I have ever met, to exchange words with the president of the United States, and to work with ethical corporate leaders like Lew Wasserman and Bob Schwartz, and dedicated public servants like John Gardner and Esther Peterson?

Now, in my eighties, I see aging as my major challenge. I recognize it as a more significant part of life than I had assumed. But I am not totally naive—there is no question aging is no panacea. Being increasingly conscious of my body's failures is inescapable, but the trick is not to allow myself to become too preoccupied with the obvious. Instead, I find joy in continuing my public interest work and focus my energies on doing what I can do in that arena. As I take more time to listen, I find I can express my love for my family and friends with a greater depth than I ever dreamed possible when I was working.

Many of my early perceptions of myself, so potent in shaping how I met life, are still with me but I have learned to cope. I am much more able to get close to people and I feel much more comfortable asserting my authority in work situations when necessary. Along with that has come a much greater sense of interdependence with my colleagues and a much greater ability to reach out for their expertise than I ever allowed myself when I was younger. I no longer fear being swallowed up if I let go.

As I age, I can see that growing up in my family had its problems but it also had its advantages. I am more willing to accept what I gained from them, inheriting my mother's energy and forthrightness, for example, and recognizing that my Aunt Rosalie and my Uncle Livy, though powerful role models, had their own personality issues. I am not certain my two sisters shared my perceptions of the family; I know they recalled different experiences, but I don't know the impact of those experiences on how they led their lives. I can only answer for myself and what I learned that enabled me to put behind me many of the myths I grew up with.

I have often wondered whether my initial attraction to the law was a psychological expression of my need to express my anger and do it in a socially acceptable way. What better profession is there to validate assertiveness and hostility and give it a legitimate outlet than going against a worthy adversary! It is probably not so strange that I left the law after my initial analysis and moved into a more policy-oriented arena that from my earliest days had always been a concern of mine. I no longer needed that outlet for my anger. I also believe my feelings about those less fortunate and my experience of being outside the main stream strongly influenced my affinity with the consumer movement and with those who are disadvantaged.

Since I retired, my family inheritance has been extremely helpful in enabling me to pursue my public service passions, where I have found my greatest joy. It's no longer important for me to try and understand where those concerns come from. A friend of mine claimed my concern for injustice was a product of a guilt complex because I came from a wealthy family. I took umbrage with that at the time but now I see it differently. It is probably true and yet is not something I am ashamed of. I do care about people who have never had my opportunities and I still want to make the world a better place. So why, I ask myself, should I quibble about where those goals came from?

Today, I am more at peace with myself and rather enjoy old age except for the physical disabilities that have recently emerged. Being older has taught me to put aside my need to be first and always in charge. I am more able to let others ask the questions. Of course, I still can't resist filling in a vacuum and still want to lead. But I enjoy working as a volunteer and being an advocate. For the first time, I can appreciate that others may be able to be more effective in a situation than I. My generation doesn't necessarily have all the best, or the only answers to issues that face society. Daily, I make a secret vow I will never be like my father and say, "In my day, we never etc. etc." I am pleased if I get the point, and hopefully am able to retreat gracefully when the occasion warrants it.

Among the joys of old age is realizing I don't need to compete as much as I did when I was young. This is personal growth on my part, but probably it's mostly due to the simple reality that I can't compete as effectively as I used to. My instinctive desire to compete—especially with the driver of the car ahead of me—or to get attention has not disappeared completely, but at least I have it more under control. I'm happy I can enjoy my friends for what they are and have learned to accept that they, like I, have their particular flaws and foibles. For too many years I expected friends to be perfect and felt rejected when they did not live up to my expectations.

At my age, and living as long as I have, I find tremendous satisfaction in seeing women in positions of prominence and their proliferation in every facet of the work place. And I take pleasure in watching them speak up with conviction, force and confidence. Society can no longer get by with viewing women as unacceptable and incompetent and relegating them to a position of second-class citizenship. No longer are they introduced as the "first" or "only;" women are an accepted part of the human scene.

Every day my personal life grows richer as my professional life grows smaller. I enjoy my Vital Aging Group, as we sixteen senior citizens continue to explore our retirement and other issues that strike our fancy. One member of the group, just widowed, has fallen in love with a widower. Another is deeply involved with global warming. One has learned to cope with an almost total loss of vision and is facilitating a low vision group and some of us have quasi-debilitating physical limitations. We discuss retirement or anything else that strikes our fancy. I see friends more, and better understand the need to take time out to keep these friendships active and fulfilling.

I hadn't been in therapy for several years, but recently went through a bout of extreme anxiety and depression, and decided to once again seek help, which has proved enormously productive. So, life continues in its familiar patterns. And once again, I continue to learn about relationships and how to ensure that my old familial demons are not getting in the way of my being the kind of person I want to be.

And I read more. At long last I no longer feel guilty about reading or doing other "frivolous" things in the middle of a day that should be devoted to "work!" Wonderful, trivial things amuse me. I am addicted to computer solitaire. My father used to play the game endlessly and that may be where I got my interest. I even dare to admit I watch afternoon reruns of *Murder She Wrote,* with Angela Lansbury. I also have the time to indulge my lifelong love of music and have a Metropolitan Opera subscription in New York, enjoying the same seats my grandmother Short had before the turn of the century.

My interest in traveling has been considerably enriched by having my good friend, Sue Whitman, travel with me. We have explored the exotic countries such as Morocco, Uzbekistan, Egypt, Israel and Vietnam, as well as most of the Europe and its major cities, such as London, Edinburgh, Glyndebourne, Paris, Brussels, Oslo, Stockholm, Copenhagen, Sicily, Leningrad and the Balkan capitals.

I decided to throw myself an eightieth birthday party, and was astounded at the response. People got up and said wonderful things about their relationship with me and what I meant to them. I had trouble taking it all in. Compliments have always been difficult for me to accept. I have always yearned for love and respect, but once I started to be able to give it, I quickly found I received it in abundance. I am not as spontaneous as I would like to be, and I still don't share enough of my feelings with my family and my friends but I have a wonderful family life and thoroughly enjoy my nephews and their families.

My delight is a summerhouse on the Chesapeake Bay that I share with my wonderful nephew, Charlie, and his family. When they lived in California, they introduced me to the camping I had never done as a child, and on my seventieth birthday they gave me a bicycle! Now, in my eighties, they've introduced me to kayaking, and I love it! I have even sailed with them in Tonga and the Caribbean. All in all, they have given me a life that I might never had had as I aged. At one point, very early in my aging process, I felt that Charlie was being too solicitous when I thought I was handling something well. When I told him about it, he said, "OK, Mary, if you will promise to ask for help when you need it, then I won't bother you." That has worked well, but more important, I have learned to ask.

I recognize how many inconsistencies I have dealt with—a rebel who ended up living with her mother until she was forty, a feminist who was never comfortable with the name, a woman who takes pride in accomplishment but never joined the woman's movement and a retiree for whom work was still the major driving force in life. Still, I don't think I would change anything in my life. Sometimes it has been difficult, but it has been a rich life—rich in professional experiences and rich in relationships with my family and friends. What I didn't have as a child has been more than compensated for by what I have been able to do as an adult.

This then is my story. Most of the walls are down now. I accept that my emotional demons will always be with me, but how I have dealt with them is, in the end, the measure of the woman I have and will become. No small triumph as I now reflect upon where it all started.

Notes

1. Madeleine Albright points this out in her book, *Madam Secretary*, p. xv.

FURTHER READING

Transcript of Oral Interview conducted on November 26, 1997 for the Woman's National Democratic Club Educational Foundation, Washington D.C. by Jewell Fenzi, chair, Oral History Project. The full transcript in hard copy ($25.00) or electronic format is available at the club from Patricia Fitzgerald, 202-232-7363 (#3003) (51 pp).

Transcript of Oral History Interview conducted on October 9 and 24, 2003 for the Federal Trade Commission by Marc Winerman, Esq. Director, Oral History Project (66 pp), available at http://www.ftc.gov/ftc/history/mgjinterview.htm

Mary Gardiner Jones Papers
Special Collections Research Center
Syracuse University Library
Syracuse NY 13244

The papers include materials from her tenure as a Federal Trade Commissioner (1964-1973). The papers are arranged in categories: General External Communications and Activities files, Intra Commission Circulations, Efforts to Introduce FTC to Strategic Planning System, Miscellaneous Printed Material, External Commission Correspondence, FTC Legal Files of Commission Opinions and Briefs, Awards and Daily Calendar, and Speeches, Articles and Taped Interviews. The papers contain material relevant to the women's and consumer movements, as well as to the Federal Trade Commission and regulatory issues.